CUL-D

Crossroads

NAVIGATING LIFE'S TWISTS AND TURNS

IN YOUR TWENTIES

WITH COURAGEOUS CLARITY

by

MARY SPENCER VEAZEY

hope*books

"*Cul-de-sac Crossroads* is a beautiful, faith-centered roadmap for women navigating life in their 20s. Through personal stories and simple action steps, Mary Spencer shows us how to find true fulfillment and purpose in a decade where we're figuring out who we are and what we want to do with our lives."

— **STEPHANIE MAY WILSON**, host of *Girls Night* podcast and author of *Create a Life You Love*

"WOW! This book is FULL of practical ways to walk with Jesus in our everyday lives. Through Mary Spencer's insightful wisdom and relatable stories, you will discover a whole new level of what it looks like to be in a personal relationship with a loving God."

— **MELISSA LEA HUGHES**, TikTok influencer and speaker

"Mary Spencer's honest description of life after college as a young Christian woman is both courageous and heartwarming. She candidly reminds the reader that living in the unknown is not easy - but that trusting in our omniscient and all-knowing God is enough to brave even the fiercest storm."

— **CAROLINE BRIDGES COOK**, author of *Hungry*

To my mom and dad. I dream bigger and love louder because of who you both are and raised me to be. Anything feels possible because, well, it just is when you grow up with parents like mine.

Details in some anecdotes and stories have been changed to protect the identities of the persons involved.

Table of Contents

Foreword

In the hustle and bustle of life, it's easy to feel lost, disconnected, or uncertain about the path ahead. But then, there are those rare souls like Mary Spencer, whose mere presence feels like a long-lost friend you've known your entire life.

It takes mere seconds in her presence to recognize her uniqueness, her authenticity, and her unwavering commitment to a mission that is nothing short of transformative. Mary Spencer is not just on a mission; she is the embodiment of a mission—a mission to empower women, to guide them through life's ups and downs, and to lead them into the abundant life that Jesus offers.

As you delve into the pages of *Cul-de-sac Crossroads*, prepare to embark on a transformative journey unlike any other. This book is not just another narrative; it is a beacon of clarity amidst the fog of uncertainty. Through her own lived experiences and storytelling, she invites us to confront our dead ends and discover that they are, in fact, gateways to new beginnings.

She speaks directly to the younger selves that reside within each of us, urging us to reclaim our dreams and embrace the abundant life that awaits. This message inside these pages is not merely a book; it is a lifeline—a lifeline that meets all walks of life, regardless of your circumstances. Whether you find yourself amidst the throes of success or grappling with the burdens of adversity, Mary Spencer's message offers guidance and the unwavering assurance that God is just getting started with you.

As I read through the pages of Mary Spencer's book, I was reminded of why her voice is not just significant but essential in today's world. She is more than an author; she is a close confidante—a fast friend whose wisdom and warmth covers you like a hug from a loved one you've been counting down the days to see.

Without a doubt, you'll quickly see that her words will invite you to step into a sense of peace, joy, and freedom that you didn't know existed. As you journey through the pages, I am confident that you will not emerge unchanged.

By the time you reach the final page, you will find that the hopelessness you carried with you at the beginning has been replaced by a sense of possibility, purpose, and a new hope... a hope found in Jesus. This hope that Mary Spencer beautifully uncovers by helping you understand your true identity is a hope that will stay with you for your entire life.

New beginnings await! Every cul-de-sac is an opportunity for a new start. Turn the page with me.

Hope Reagan Harris

Author, Speaker, and Founder of
Purpose Doesn't Pause Inc.

Introduction

THE CUL-DE-SAC

I grew up at the end of a cul-de-sac with oak trees older than my great-grandmother decorating every side of our brick house with green shutters. When I picture heaven, it looks a lot like our backyard: full of azaleas and surrounded by glimmering water beckoning you to take a dip in its cool liquid. A couple of springer spaniels are usually bouncing around the yard attempting to hunt squirrels but somehow, they haven't found success yet.

Our road wasn't a road you typically turned down. With only four houses on our street, you came down either very lost or with great purpose, with not much in between. Once, there was a dead-end sign at the beginning of our street, but someone stole it along the way, never to be replaced.

I've walked, skated, biked, ran, and driven all up and down that sweet street over the past decade, almost two. At the end of the road was where I lived a lot of my life. I'd come back home each day, reset, and start again.

Cul-de-sac is a fancy little word for a dead end, but at the end of the street is where my life began. Only those with little imagination view cul-de-sacs as dead ends. Cul-de-sacs are an opportunity for a new direction, while dead ends leave you with nowhere to go, and no way to move forward. You can loop around a cul-de-sac and choose a new destination, but a dead end has you slamming on your breaks, confused as to why the street ends here.

I don't want a life that feels like dead end after dead end. I want a life and a heart that believes redirection can be what's best for me if needed. But throughout my 20s, life has stretched and squeezed me to a point where I felt like I wouldn't be able to get out of the place that I was in, stuck at the end of the road.

My life has drastically changed over the past 2 years, and I see how God has been gracious enough to get me out of that dead end over and over again. He's bringing me to a new crossroads, showing me the options and abundance He has for me.

I wrote this book for you and for me too. I wrote it for the younger version of myself at the end of that cul-de-sac. She was always a dreamer, escaping to a different world through books and her imagination. There was no such thing as a dead end, only cul-de-sacs with new directions and perspectives. But as I got older, the rose-colored glasses faded into the world's reality of darkness and dead ends. I don't want it to be that way, though.

As advanced as technology is, Google Maps has yet to provide me with a roadmap on how to navigate life in your 20s. No one is talking about it before it's right up in your face: your 20s are HARD. It is the first time in your life when everyone your age is in a different stage of life.

Married friends, single friends, divorced friends, friends with babies, friends with houses, friends with high-paying jobs, friends barely able to pay the bills. Amid all of the crazy stages of this decade, I know for certain there is something special about our 20s. I've stepped into my own during this decade of life. What do I like? Who do I like? Where do I want to live in the world? What matters to me?

I know life will continue to fluctuate, but I want some rhythms that will stay consistent. I want a deep relationship with Jesus. I want to feel confident in my purpose and what I spend my days doing. I want to care for my friends well and with intention.

When I landed this book deal, I was ecstatic. I knew how important this topic was because I wished for a resource about my 20s from a faith perspective, but I couldn't find it.

So I wrote it instead. But I worried what people would think. Why would I think I could do this?

I have to keep turning out of that dead end in my mind. I get to choose what happens at this crossroad: I can stop here or I can redirect to where I'm needed, where God is leading me.

Take my hand, jump into my car, smile, and wave to the little brunette child with a bob, roller skates, and a lime green iPod nano that's standing at the end of the cul-de-sac. My cul-de-sac. You wave to your younger self too. They are proud of us and where we are headed.

Being in your 20s is hard. But it is so much sweeter once we discover who we are and what our purpose is in this messy world. Those little girls are smiling with snaggle-tooth smiles admiring how far you and I have already come and where this adventure will hopefully lead by the end of this book. Ready, friend? Let's jump in.

P.S. At the end of the book, I have written some discussion questions for you to reflect on by yourself, with your Bible study, with a group of friends, or whoever else you might want to read this book with. Sometimes I find it helpful to have discussion questions to further dive into the topic at hand, other times I just want to read a book and skip any questions altogether. It's totally up to you!

Crossroad 1

WHOSE YOU ARE

As a child, my friends and I would wait patiently (and sometimes not so patiently) for our parents to arrive at school to pick us up. My friends and I would sit together in the hallway, searching the sea of cars driving up looking for the one we belonged to. Finally, we'd see them: a mother, father, family friend, or guardian. I would feel a jolt of joy when my name was called, announcing that my mom or dad was here and it was time for me to go home. We would race down the hall and into the car of the one taking us home, babbling about our day.

Kids know who they belong to. They are becoming more and more like the ones that they interact with the most. They know who they belong to before they know who they really are.

I wasn't standing on solid ground for a long time when it came to *who* I was. I didn't understand how much that deeply matters and changes everything. It sets the groundwork for who I am and what I'll do with this one, deeply precious life that I have.

This first section, I hope, will point you home to Jesus. He's laid the foundation for a safe home and space to get to know Him, which will, in turn, lead you to know yourself better too. That childlike faith can work wonders, and I'm already awestruck with what He hasn't done yet.

Chapter 1

GETTING LOW ENOUGH TO GET JESUS

I n the crumbly little lot of my shoe-box freshman dorm, I sat in my car with my face in my hands, grieving what I had done. Could someone remind me why I had chosen to go to college out-of-state, where I did not know a single soul? I had grown up in South Georgia and moved to Auburn, Alabama, only 3 hours away from my hometown, but it might as well have been Mars. The coming-of-age movies made it look so glamorous leaving your hometown behind for a fresh start. You are supposed to get the life you always dreamed of but never had in high school.

So far, my new chapter of life included getting cut from most of the sororities during recruitment week, breaking up with my high school boyfriend, and not having a single friend nearby to talk to.

I had come to know Jesus at a pretty young age and had always believed in Him and what He had done for me, but I didn't fully grasp what it was like to have a relationship with Jesus until this very moment, where parts of my old life were ceasing to exist and the beginning of my college experience was full of dead ends.

Tearfully, I asked God, sitting in my tiny two-door car, to meet me there, in the parking lot of Dunn Hall. I'd give everything to Him if He'd just show me peace and joy like I'd never known before. I wanted that desperately.

Toward the end of high school, I struggled to feel like I fit in anywhere, and I thought college would be the answer to my problems. But at this point, it was proving to be the opposite. All I had been hoping for was true joy and contentment, but I had yet to find it.

After I sat there talking to God, hoping He was actually listening, I felt a sliver of peace wash over me. I didn't know how or if it was going to be okay, but it felt like it might be. It felt like the first time I'd fully surrendered to what God's plan might be for my life.

I wish everything changed that day, and I became the happiest person in the world overnight, but that is not exactly what happened. God took me low enough to get me out of my own way and where I could see nothing but Him. I didn't have any friends in Auburn at this point, sorority recruitment had been a terrible experience, and my relationship was over... I made it seem like all rainbows and sunshine to the social media world, but I was crying myself to sleep many nights during those first few months at college, even after me and Jesus met in my car that gloomy night.

When I felt like I was at such a low point, I had nothing and no one to cling to besides my faith. I had to learn to return to that over and over again, daily, hourly, minute by minute, to find peace in the biggest and smallest moments of my life. I can easily find myself swept up in everything but what matters, and I started grasping that during those first few months at Auburn. My 18-year-old self didn't recognize it yet, but I craved control over every detail of my life. (Welcome to the life of an Enneagram 8 woman.)

Life comes at ya quickly, and now I'm no longer that freshman child and am instead a 26-year-old with a job and an apartment and am learning every day how in the world to do this adult thing.

One of my least favorite adult responsibilities so far is doctor's appointments. Insurance is one of the most mind-boggling monsters I've encountered. Doctor's appointments as an adult feel like I'm 17 again getting my oil changed for the first time. Do I need my air filters cleaned out? What kind of oil do I need? Am I going to be taken advantage of to pay for things I don't need?

Last week, I went to the optometrist. It's been over a decade since I've gone to get my eyes checked. Oops. I am trying with every fiber of my being to avoid contacts. I do not want them. I don't want glasses either, but recently on a long road trip, I noticed my eyes hurt and were so blurry as I looked at the cars up ahead. That didn't feel like a great sign. My left eye also has been twitching pretty consistently for the better part of the year, so I reluctantly Googled "eye doctors in Nashville" and set up an appointment.

I'd also like to say that I think if I had known that you can now pay a little extra and not get your eyes dilated and instead get these wild pictures of your eyes taken, then I probably would have called a long time ago. Why is no one talking about this phenomenon?

I digress. When I asked the doctor why my left eye always twitches, she responded with: "Do you get enough sleep? Do you drink too much caffeine? Are you stressed?"

Did she have to be so up in my business? As if I didn't already know these things, having a stranger point them out to me made me hear her loud and clear.

My eye doctor told me I should wear my glasses at work and while driving as well. My vision is deteriorating a little bit, and I have a resource readily available to help me with my vision. Why didn't I want to take advantage of it? I couldn't keep waiting to do something about my vision, it was quickly changing for the worse and I didn't want to wait until it got as bad as it could get.

As I sat there in the chair talking with the optometrist about my options, I thought about how I see Jesus better in the blurriest, lowest moments of my life. I am working every day to get close to a 20/20 vision with Him, but sometimes I get in the way of my own self. I see pain as a product of God's lack of love for me, but He is allowing me to get to know Him better and cling to Him a little more tightly through hurt and hard times.

I'm nearsighted when it comes to my faith, and I'm starting to think that's a good thing. I don't need to be able to see what's going to happen 100 yards down the road in my life. I need to focus on what's right in front of me, for today.

I need Jesus. I need resources and people in my life that point me to Jesus. I need a little help to get back to as close as I can get to a perfect vision because, from my point of view, some of my life is distorted.

Without knowing who I am in Him, I do not know who I am. Before I deeply and thoughtfully knew Jesus and sought a relationship with Him, I was without direction or a clear purpose. But my eyes are sharpening with a laser focus on my Savior.

We need the foundation of a relationship with Him, or else we are unable to become who we are and who we are going to be.

———

Yesterday, I was driving back to Nashville from my hometown of Tifton, Georgia. Along the way, I was surprised to see snow fluttering around as I drove through Chattanooga. It covered the ground in its snowy magic, and the trees were dusted with a thin layer of white. As a kid from South Georgia, this was a sight to behold.

But about thirty minutes into the snow, it became extremely foggy. The worst fog I've driven through in a long time. I couldn't see more than ten or so yards ahead of me. I started feeling slightly worried. How long would this go on? Where did this come from, and why now? What should I do?

But then it hit me: I just needed to see what was right in front of me to keep going.

On that very same drive, I was listening to a Jennie Allen podcast titled, "Don't Overcomplicate Jesus." Well, as I do with many other areas in my life, I tend to overcomplicate every part of my faith. I read too much into what does or doesn't happen. I get confused when people fight over what their interpretation of the Bible is. I feel anxious about the future and regretful of my past.

Jesus is asking you and me to stop making His love for us so complicated. God sent His Son to die on the cross for our sins. He bore the weight of the world and our sin. God gives us the gift of new and eternal life freely. No strings attached. All you have to do is surrender to Him and believe.

He loves us. He sets us free. He redeems our story. He is listening. He is crafting our future far better and brighter than we ever could have dreamed. So amid the fog, I'm grateful for the clarity of seeing just the next step ahead of me. That's all we really need.

You may have grown up in the church and been burned. You might have lost a parent at a young age and lost faith that God could be real and could be good. Maybe you've watched people in your life say they love Jesus, but their actions don't reflect what they claim to be true in their lives.

If you are unsure about what faith in Jesus really is and if that's even something you want to be a part of, I completely understand. My hope through this first section is to get clear on who Jesus actually is and why faith matters. I don't mind if you don't see eye to eye with me. I've got friends of all different backgrounds and beliefs and am so grateful for all of their perspectives. All I want to do is show Jesus for who He truly is, not portrayed as who the world has made Him look like at times or through the reputations Christians may have because broken people make up the church.

———

I used to work for a faith-based addiction treatment center for women. Daily, I would hear women tell story after story of how they lost bits and pieces of who they were because they placed alcohol or drugs on the pedestal of their lives. Mother's Day was a really hard day for the clients. No mother wants to be away from their kids on Mother's Day, and we had to constantly remind the clients that by being in treatment, they were taking steps to become the best mothers they could be moving forward.

One year, we had a church partner give the clients colorful stationery, pens, and stamps with hearts on them to write to their kids and/or their moms for Mother's Day, which touched my and the client's hearts. I can't tell you how much it meant to the women to be able to write home. I went downstairs to hang out with the clients while they were completing this activity, and I struck up a conversation with one of the women decorating a card.

Diane is a mother, probably early 50s. She went to treatment in California many years ago and was clean for a long time until she got back together with an ex-boyfriend who was in active addiction. She started using again and realized that she was headed back into the cycle of addiction and knew she had to remove herself from this situation.

So Diane packed a bag and got on a Greyhound and decided to move to Georgia. She had no connections in Georgia, but she didn't want any. She didn't want the chance of hopping back in with old friends who could persuade her to keep her addiction alive.

My new friend also packed several bottles of alcohol in her bag on the Greyhound. She couldn't bring herself to stop, so she kept secretly drinking on the bus.

A man approached her and asked if he could sit with her on the bus. He seemed nice enough, so she allowed him to sit with her. He became her friend, asking polite questions and trying his best to get to know her.

Once he felt like he had earned her trust, he decided to tell her that he knew what she was doing: she was drinking on the bus and couldn't bring herself to stop. He told her he had once been in her shoes; he was now in recovery.

Neither of them was planning to get off the bus in Nashville, but her new friend told her they needed to get off the bus so he could take her to the hospital. So they got off the bus, went to the hospital and Diane was then able to come into our care.

As she told me this story, I was amazed. The kindness of a stranger to stop and notice his surroundings, realize she needed help, and build a friendship with her resonated with me. He wasn't quick to point fingers or shame her. He saw a stranger and became her friend. He did what no one in her life had done before: He laid down his plans to launch her into freedom. This man reminded me a lot of the character of Jesus, willing to leave his plans behind to help another person. At one of the lowest moments of Diane's life, she was able to recognize that she needed help through the friendship of a stranger, and now her life has changed because of it.

We often told clients seeking sobriety that the opposite of addiction is not sobriety. The opposite of addiction is connection. Weaving your life together with others brings you hope, joy, accountability, and friends that become family. What we place on the pedestal of our lives defines who we are.

What I've found over the years is that the moments that God is at the center of all that I do, I feel fulfilled, hopeful, and surprised by what I can accomplish and who I surround myself with. Even in really hard seasons, I feel a fire of purpose and connectivity to myself and who's around me.

When that pedestal shifts to work or friends or money or what I do or don't have, I feel bits of myself slipping. I begin to isolate and disconnect.

My friends who are in recovery will tell you and me over and over that connection changes everything. Getting a sponsor, going to AA or NA meetings, and living in a community that is in recovery are all keys to changing their lives forever. They will tell you that you must change your people, places, and things to become well and stay well. Who we are around and where we spend our time affects the way we mold our lives. They'll also tell you that in their AA meetings, they often talk about a higher power. For some that's Jesus. They cling to their faith when they don't know how they'll go a day without drinking. They cling to their faith when they relapse and have to start again on day one. They cling to their faith as recovery is not linear.

Often, we meet Jesus when we hit rock bottom. At least that's how it was for me. That's how it's been for some of my friends who are now in recovery and have found faith in Jesus. We're learning what it means to trust in Him when we are lower than we've ever been. It hurts, but He redeems.

———

Lately, I feel like I've been taking one step forward and two steps back in my faith. I'm not mad at God. I've just seen so much brokenness in the world lately that I feel frustrated. My Nashville community has recently been devastated and heartbroken after a school shooting. I've heard about so many school shootings in the news over the years, but it burns in a new way when it happens a few miles from your home.

I also have two people I love dearly who are currently recovering from battles with cancer. It's hard to see the good on so many dark days. Why is God allowing all of this?

Gray areas drive me crazy; I'm searching for black-and-white pictures of life's problems. Uncertainty either leads to open hands or clenched fists, and God can't free me or bless me if I am not willing to trust Him.

Sometimes we need a change of environment, but maybe what I really need is a change of heart within me. God can't fully use me for His glory if I close myself off to the possibilities of paths ahead. So maybe I'll try to allow God to control my steps, moving toward a path I've never traveled down before. Trying, desperately trying, to trust Him in the midst of so much heartbreak.

I want to get low enough to get to know Jesus for who He is, not from the variety of definitions people have told me, but for who I see in the Bible and the ways He's working in my life and bringing it together in a way I could not do on my own. I want to see if you and I know Jesus for who He actually is and pursue what He really wants for us. Could it be a life that leaves us filled up in a world that drains us daily?

———

Behind my parent's house is a big pond.... or a small lake. Depends on the way you view it. I moved into that house surrounded on three sides by water when I was in elementary school. To be able to jump in and swim whenever we want was the biggest highlight of each summer. We used to go tubing just about every single afternoon, letting my dad sling us off the tube over and over and over. It's a wonder we all survived those tubing adventures.

Over time, the idea of swimming in the lake became less and less inviting. I began to recognize how murky the waters were and would think about the possibility of snakes or other creatures lurking below, waiting for us to jump in. I didn't like what I couldn't see.

When along the way did I lose this childlike faith to jump in, not knowing what I couldn't see... and not caring? I just trusted it would be fine and, more importantly, that it would be fun.

Do you ever think about the faith you had as a child? The faith you had in your parents to take care of you; the faith that you had in Jesus; the faith you had in some consistency in schedule with school or family. Or maybe you had none of that. Maybe over time, you grew to lack faith in your family or didn't begin to know Jesus from a young age.

Trusting the Lord is like getting in that murky lake. I trust even though I can't see what's below. I can't control my circumstances, but I can control the way I react. I can cannonball into the waters trusting the Lord will be my life vest. He won't let me sink.

Maybe next time I go home, I'll jump into the lake without overthinking it. Not honing in on the bad, but rather focusing on letting my soul be a little freer. And I'll remember the ways the Lord has set me free. I won't forget the ways and moments I've been lower than I've ever been. He's there, time and time again, picking me up and reminding me who I am. And I'll take back my childlike faith in the waters that glitter like diamonds in the sun.

Chapter 2

SPENDING TIME
WITH JESUS

My to-do list is always a mile longer than the number of hours that exist in a given day. It's funny how that works. Every single day I overestimate what I can get done, and I usually wait to spend time with Jesus after I get a lot of my list done for the day. I swear I am well-intentioned. I reason that once I have completed all the tasks on my to-do list, I won't be preoccupied with thoughts about what I need to get done.

That would be great in a perfect world, but after 26 years of living, I've come to the shocking realization that my system is not working for me. I throw in a quick devotional here and there and read my Bible when I can, but I'm not sitting down and spending time with Jesus. I want to, I really do, but I have a hard time focusing when I feel like I need to get so much done.

In the mornings before work, I love to go for a mile walk to wake myself up. I do it almost every morning, sauntering around my neighborhood soaking up the sunshine peeking over the horizon and the birds chirping their morning hellos to me before the rest of the world wakes up. After my walk, I try to squeeze in time in the Word, rarely succeeding, often rushing through. I've been trying to switch things up lately, though. Instead of walking first and then spending time with Jesus second, what if I switched the order? Monumental idea, I know.

I plopped down at my wooden desk, opened up my Bible to the book of Matthew, and began my Precept Study. I sat there with Jesus, didn't rush a moment, and it changed the trajectory of my day. Not doing a single thing before spending time with Jesus changed the way I walked throughout my daily routine.

Moving my priorities realigned my heart for what actually needed to be accomplished for the day, and that left me feeling like what I had done for the day was enough... until I got into my old ways again and forgot how good it felt to start my day with Jesus.

But here we are– it's September 2023, and I have COVID. Again.

I started not feeling 100% yesterday afternoon, but as a girl with seasonal allergies, I didn't think twice about it. The first event I had planned at my new job was happening this weekend, and I was so excited to meet some new people and watch this event I had planned come to life.

I went and grabbed some COVID tests at Walgreens after work and told myself I'd test just to be safe. I pulled out those tests as soon as I got home, and I waited for the results. I didn't have to wait long, though, because about two minutes in, I saw what I feared: a positive sign.

Now on my wild and crazy Friday night, I am sitting on my balcony in my wooden oversized chair with a comfy cream cushion. Twinkly bright lights illuminate my little nook of the world as I breathe in the seventy-degree air (well, as much breathing as I can do anyway) and write to you. I just wrote 958 really good words that I was so excited about, but for some reason, Google Docs decided to further ruin my day and delete 721 of them when my screen refreshed. But I'm fine. It's fine. We're fine. I'm not counting.

Anyway. I have felt overwhelmed with busyness lately, and in some ways, I'm taking this as God's not-so-gentle way of telling me I need some rest. Badly. And some patience. Maybe all of those words I thought were good needed to be deleted. Another gentle nudge that I am not in control and any good words I write aren't really mine anyway.

I've struggled with people-pleasing the past few months too. I'm not sure if it's because I'm at a new job and I want to do well or if it's the insecurity my last job left me with after some pretty sour situations. Maybe I'm having a bit of imposter syndrome writing a book and feeling like I can't do this deep down.

It's all of it. So here I am with nothing to do. I have already finished a whole season of *Selling the OC* today, and now it's 8 pm and I've decided to spend time with Jesus since I can't be at the event that I planned.

I opened up my Bible to Matthew 13:3-9 where Jesus talks about the parable of the sower. I have read this passage so many times, but tonight in the midst of having no other choice but to slow down I heard these verses in a new way.

The sower tries scattering seeds in all sorts of different places: a path, rocky ground, among thorns, and on good soil. The seed dropped along the path is quickly destroyed. The seed on rocky ground sprouts up, but the lack of depth in the soil leaves the seed dying as quickly as it sprouted. The seed that fell among thorns could not grow in those conditions.

But then good soil came onto the scene. Amid such richness, the seed took root and produced more than the sower could have imagined.

I come from a family of farmers. I grew up toddling around watermelon fields where America's favorite 4th of July fruit sprung up from the soil and blessed all of our souls with flavor and memories attached to this sweet treat. We grew peanuts and the snow of the South too: fluffy, white cotton that covered acres and acres of land.

Good years and bad years in farming are unpredictable due to external factors. Droughts leave the soil dry as an Arizona desert. Late spring freezes wipe out crops so close to being ready to harvest, devastating farmers and their families. External factors can't be controlled, but what can be controlled is the condition of the soil when we plant seeds.

I have been somewhere bouncing back and forth between allowing God's Word to take root on rocky ground and in good soil. In the rush of my life, I see the rocky ground as an easy way out. The fruit of my labor springs to life quickly, but it dies just as swiftly as it sprouted.

The difference between that rocky ground and good soil is the distinction between a believer and a disciple. Believing in Jesus and following Jesus are not the same. One breeds heart change and the other produces life change from the inside out.

I don't want to just be a believer; I want to be a disciple. I want to seek out Jesus, know Him, and know my purpose more fully. I want to be just as much of a good steward of the heart I've been given, even when the rocky ground feels like the more convenient place to plant roots.

Good fruit doesn't just happen. Rich soil isn't always easy to find, and it's not always found in the same places year after year. Good fruit requires intentionality. When we don't do our homework on what good soil is, it can devastate not only our lives but those around us. And we need to bear fruit, not only for our sake but for the sake of others. When we're healthy, we model health for those around us too.

As I continued spending time with Jesus on my twinkly-lit porch, I read some other verses that connected to what I was reading. John 15:1-8 shows that without the vine, there are no branches for fruit to grow from. We need the vine, and we have to abide in the one true Vine to see fruit in our lives. Sometimes the fruit doesn't look like what we thought we planted, and that frustrates me to no end... until I see His promises come true. He knows better, and by abiding in Him and seeking out His Word, I know Him better. Diving into who He is allows me to know *whose* I am and, in turn, *who* I am.

The condition of our hearts affects the condition of our fruit. By making room for the Lord to work and clearing out the weeds, we open up ourselves to live a life that is fulfilling and on fire for the Gospel.

I want to rush through the fruit growing. It's uncomfortable, and quite frankly, I've got things to do, but I feel God tugging on my sleeves, begging that I take life one step at a time with Him instead of trying to rush ahead of what He has for me today.

We have to root ourselves in the Word He's given us because it changes us from the inside out. Our hearts are consuming an overload of information daily that sprouts weeds all around the roots and fruits we're trying to grow, so we have to return to Him daily, hourly, minute by minute. Tonight sitting here on my patio, I find myself reminded of what it's like to spend time with Jesus. Time with Him that isn't rushed leaves a margin for the Lord to speak to me.

———

I remember at summer camp as a kid, we would divide up into teams and play a game of tug-of-war. Was I ever the strongest kid on the team? Not a chance, but I could get scrappy if I wanted to. I'm not ever going down without a fight. I'd pull on that cream-colored rope until my hands burned and my body hit the ground.

God and I go back and forth in this tug-of-war with control. He's always going to win, yes I know that, but somehow I find myself face down in the mud clinging to a rope that has been pulled to a side I wasn't prepared to cross.

We've been talking about this a lot lately, God and I, about why I don't trust Him enough to know He has my best interests at heart.

I swear I'm trying.

I've felt my soul tugging in two directions, and I want God to tell me what's going on. I can get on board if I know where we're going.

I had many moments last year where I opened my Bible and went to church just because I felt like I needed to and not because I wanted to. I think going even when you don't feel like it can often be good, but I know God's desire is for me to *want* to spend time with Him.

Growing up, I'm sure I read parts of the book of Matthew lots of times. A few years ago, I even read through the Gospels several times over many months, but it wasn't until recently that I learned something new in this story of Jesus' life that I have not been able to stop thinking about.

When Jesus has The Last Supper with the disciples, He tells them that one of them will betray Him. One by one, each disciple asked, "Is it I, Lord?"

All except one disciple, that is, asked Him that.

Judas' response was, "Is it I, Rabbi?"

Jesus was not Lord in Judas' life. He was a Rabbi, a Jewish scholar/teacher. Judas did not see Jesus as someone to worship, he saw Jesus as just another Jewish teacher.

I don't want Jesus to just be a teacher in my life, although sometimes that is what I treat Him as. I want Him to be Lord.

I don't want to be willing to betray His love, His will, His plan. I want to have Him on the throne of my heart and quit this boxing match where it's really just me vs. me.

When it was evening, he reclined at the table with the twelve. And as they were eating, he said, "Truly, I say to you, one of you will betray me." And they were very sorrowful and began to say to him one after another, "Is it I, Lord?" He answered, "He who has dipped his hand in the dish with me will betray me.

The Son of Man goes as it is written of him, but woe to that man by whom the Son of Man is betrayed! It would have been better for that man if he had not been born." Judas, who would betray him, answered, "Is it I, Rabbi?" He said to him, "You have said so."

– Matthew 26:20-25

If we seek God out as the personal Lord of our lives, it shifts everything in us: what and who we turn to for comfort, what decisions we make, and how we navigate our lives with courageous clarity. He's here, alive, and so much more than a teacher. He's my greatest friend and Savior. We're on the same team, tugging the rope from darkness into light. Furious, glorious, beaming light.

You may be skeptical about this whole Jesus thing. And that's okay. I'm glad you're here whether or not you believe what I believe. I know there are a thousand reasons and ways you may not trust God or the people in your life who are Christians.

Regardless of what you do or don't believe, you are welcome and safe here. I just want you to know and see that Jesus is so much more than I can put into words. Spending time with Jesus is how I came to know Him for myself, by diving into His Word and finding out for myself what I believe.

I want to be an independent thinker and draw conclusions about what I know to be true through Scripture and strengthen my relationship with Jesus. Every question I have ever had, every doubt that has bloomed in my mind, has always been disproven by what I read in the Bible. I don't understand everything, and sometimes I read the Bible, and I am like, "Um, hello, God? What in the world is happening?!?!" (i.e. all of Leviticus). But every time I question what is true, I find myself at the feet of Jesus, and my doubts slowly start to lift. Making Him the Lord of my life means carving out that time, so I can better hear, know, and follow Him. I hope we'll find each other there.

––––––

A common misconception is that the only way to spend valuable time with Jesus is to open up your Bible for an hour and read His Word. We learn firsthand more of who God is by reading the Bible and talking to Jesus in prayer, but for me, it's sometimes helpful to hear from someone else, whether it's reading a devotional or listening to worship music.

Music can shift our hearts. Think about your favorite songs. What emotions do they evoke from you? Every song you listen to feeds your soul something whether it evokes a laugh or smile, takes you to a dark place, or reminds you of a friend or old memory. I have a handful of worship songs that move me to tears. The words and the melodies draw out something in my heart that I can't quite explain.

A pastor at my church put it this way, "Singing is transformative in moving our heart from one place to another. Sometimes we sing *from* our heart, and other times, we sing *to* our heart. Singing pushes back the darkness in our lives."

I feel that deeply in all aspects of my life. At times, I fully mean and believe what I'm saying and hearing, but other times I am reading God's Word or singing a song of worship, reminding myself of what is true and to not give up on hope, true everlasting hope.

And maybe you're like me, and you need a guide. I am unfortunately not the type of person who can just open up the Bible and know exactly where to turn and what to study for the day without a little bit of guidance.

Buy a Bible study covering a topic or book of the Bible and walk through it daily. Find some friends who will join in with you and study God's Word together. Refresh your rhythm of how you spend time with Jesus or start for the very first time. One way isn't the only way when it comes to getting to know Jesus better.

I always hear people say that you need to pick a time of day and stick to it for your time with Jesus, but sometimes every single day looks different for me. I've had to learn to not beat myself up if I only have 15 minutes to spend with Jesus. It doesn't seem like Jesus is as interested in the *quantity* of time with Him as much as the *quality* of time with Him.

Be proud that you're spending time out of your busy day with Him. You're making room for Jesus to be invited into your life, every crevice of it, day by day, and it deeply matters. Spending time with Jesus has the power to change us from the inside out, molding us more into who He created us to be.

Chapter 3

GRANDMOTHERS WHO PRAY

I have been lucky enough in life to have four women that were and are grandmothers to me: my Nana who went to be with Jesus when I was three, my Meme who is 80 and as beautiful as ever, Ms. Peggy who worked with my dad for decades and became a part of our family early on, showering me in love from the day I was born, and Ms. Melba aka Grams, my dear grandmother who married my Papa years after my Nana passed away. Grams turned 96 this week. She still drives her Buick all over Ocilla, Georgia, running that city like she is the mayor of it. And she is. I know the citizens of Ocilla will agree.

So, I have four grandmothers. I am lucky enough to have known all of my grandmothers and to still have three out of the four alive and in really, really good shape. It is a blessing that I don't take for granted.

When I think about each of my grandmothers, the first thought that comes to mind is how they are all prayer warriors. I get cards in the mail from Meme about how she is praying for me. I get texts from Ms. Peggy randomly throughout the year as she thinks of me in her prayers. I talk to Grams on the phone and she tells me how she prays for me each day.

Grandmothers who pray are such a gift. I am sitting here at my little bistro table in my tiny apartment with tears running a stream down my face with gratitude to have grandmothers who model prayer and how much love comes with those prayers.

I have two reminders of those daily prayers from my grandmothers sitting on my ivory wicker cabinets in my apartment. One of those reminders is a beautiful angel figurine with gold wings and a gold heart in her hands. At the bottom, the words "love you more" are inscribed. Grams gave that to me and told me that she wanted it to sit in my house as a reminder that she was constantly praying for me.

The second reminder Meme gave to me as a reminder of her prayers for me is a small wooden rectangular canvas that says in black script font, "God is watching over you. I know because I asked Him to." I walk by those two physical reminders every day, and I often take for granted how special it is to have people going to the Lord in prayer on my behalf.

Prayer has always been something I couldn't quite figure out. Am I doing this right? Is God really listening? Are my prayers too self-centered? What could I ask for? But then I am reminded of my grandmothers. They grew up in a time when there was little technology. A million resources were not available at their fingertips. Prayer could not be overly complicated because there wasn't a reason or way for it to be.

It's always been a conversation with God. No right or wrong way, just a way. The Way.

Almost two years ago, I started recognizing that I was praying for specific things and then not really thinking much about whether or not God answered my prayer. If He answered my prayer, I would be happy about it for five minutes, saying, "Thanks, God!" and then move on to the next item on my list. It left me feeling like God wasn't doing much when in reality I wasn't opening my eyes to all that He was doing around me. I was taking way too much credit for how my prayers were answered, and I began to realize it wasn't about me even a little bit.

I wasn't sure how I could recognize God answering my prayers in a tangible way where I wouldn't and couldn't forget what He was doing for me. I love to journal, but I'm not one who frequently reviews what I've written in my journal. I usually write out all of my feelings and then turn the page and keep moving, so that didn't feel like the right answer. I opened up my desk one day and saw an array of rainbow sticky notes and thought, "What if I just stick up my prayers on my wall?"

I wrote down a handful of prayers I had been praying that could have tangible answers one way or another, put the day's date on them, taped them up on my wall, and prayed for what I had written on those notes as I passed by them. When a prayer was answered, regardless of the outcome being what I wanted or not, I would get a second sticky note, write down how God answered that prayer, put the date on it, stick the two together, and move them to the opposite side of my wall. One by one, I watched the sticky notes stack up on the right side with answered prayers.

Sometimes, God answered the prayers exactly like I hoped He would. Other times the answers weren't what I wanted, but regardless, He did answer. Something about seeing over and over the ways God was hearing me and listening to my prayers gave me a little bit more faith each time it happened.

My church is going through Psalms this summer and how Psalms are and can be our guide for prayer. We're only a week in, but as I've been going through the suggested reading for each day I've been blown away by how applicable it's been to so many scenarios that have happened throughout my week. Psalms give us the words to praise God and pray to Him as well. We don't always have to come up with our own prayers; we can take Scripture and pray that back to God too.

Our church has also been walking through the Lord's Prayer where Jesus says the following:

"Pray then like this: Our Father in heaven, hallowed be your name. Your kingdom come, your will be done, on Earth as it is in heaven. Give us this day our daily bread, and forgive us our debts, as we also have forgiven our debtors. And lead us not into temptation, but deliver us from evil."

– Matthew 6:9-13

I can't remember a time when I didn't know this prayer. I've heard and said it so many times growing up that I didn't think about the impact of what I was saying over and over until we walked line by line through it this summer. Here's what I feel like I learned:

Our Father in heaven, hallowed be your name. We revere, respect, and sit back in awe of who God is and how holy His name is. I've been convicted recently about this. Jewish scribes used to get a new pen every time they wrote the Lord's name out of reverence for who He is and now we live in an "omg" culture. I casually throw the Lord's name around without any reverence. I want that to change.

Your kingdom come, your will be done, on Earth as it is in heaven. We submit to God's will, trusting He knows best, releasing our plans, and exchanging them for His plans. We want heaven to rain down. We want to live lives that mirror the way Jesus lived.

Give us this day our daily bread, and forgive us our debts, as we also have forgiven our debtors. I think a lot about the future. How much should I be saving for the hypothetical house, the hypothetical kids, and the hypothetical needs that I hypothetically have? Will God show up? Will I have enough? Will I be enough?

But Jesus. He says to pray for my daily bread, my daily portion. Emphasis on the *daily*. He isn't suggesting to pray for the bread I'm going to need in 2030. Sometimes I mistake bread for briars assuming God might betray me instead of bless me. He might place thorns in my hand instead of my daily bread.

But Jesus. His hands are scarred from the nails that held Him to the cross, and mine are full of daily bread. Enough for the day. I'll keep asking and praying and hoping and believing for what I need to be enough, no more, no less.

And lead us not into temptation, but deliver us from evil. We ask the Lord for His protection and peace as we walk into each day. Whether you're a palliative care nurse, a mom, a first-grade teacher, or a grad student, you see broken people and moments daily. We are those broken people too. We ask God for His strength to get us through our days.

I've overcomplicated what it means to talk to God, and the Lord's Prayer gives me a foundation for prayer, especially when I can't find the words. He's given us what we needed all along to talk to Him.

———

At my first job out of grad school, I worked for a faith-based nonprofit and I had an incredible boss named Kate (who you'll meet again in the chapter about mentors). She is a woman full of faith and would give each person in our department a half day of prayer twice a year on the clock. I had never heard of such a work perk, and I was over the moon when it came time for my first half-day of prayer.

I planned ahead of time some things I wanted to pray through and Googled ideas on how to spend four hours of prayer by myself because I honestly had no clue. I don't remember a time when I spent more than maybe fifteen minutes in prayer... if that. So I printed out a picture of the One Hour Prayer Cycle[1] and packed it in my backpack along with my Bible and my journal.

One of my boss's stipulations for my day of prayer was that it couldn't be at my house. I wasn't sure where I'd go in Nashville that would be quiet and peaceful. I quickly ruled out any coffee shop spots as I am an avid people watcher and easily distracted by the chatter around me. Since I moved to Nashville, a favorite walking spot of mine has been Radnor Lake, a massive state park nestled right outside the city. The first time I went, I couldn't believe there was this oasis in a city as big as Nashville. It does my small-town heart some good getting out to a place that feels so removed from the hustle of city life.

Radnor feels like home, so I decided there wouldn't be a better place to spend my half day of prayer than at Radnor Lake. The beauty of Radnor always rattles my soul with the reminder of how God created such beauty for us to enjoy, a small slice of heaven in the world.

I headed out to Radnor Lake bright and early and threw my pink and blue striped picnic blanket down over a wooden bench on a dock overlooking the water. It was a stunning summer morning after a long, long winter. Honeysuckles bloomed all around, filling the woods with their sweet, summer scent. The sun was peeking through the trees and its rays beat down, dancing across the water.

I began to unpack all of my belongings and started my way through the One Hour Prayer Cycle. As I followed the prayer cycle, I listened to God more than I think I ever have in my life. The prayer cycle is in 5-minute increments and you start with praise first. You keep moving through all the different steps until the hour is up. And it flies by so fast. You get to spend time in the Word, listening to Him, and so much more. (PS, this is the prayer cycle I followed!)

I confessed a lot to God while I sat there. I hadn't been prioritizing Him. I had forgotten what a gift each step we take is. I recognized while I sat on that dock how slowly some people sauntered along while I sped my way through every moment.

I realized how grateful I was for what I had in my life. I was grateful for my job. I was grateful for my co-workers. I was grateful for my relationship with Jesus.

I began praying through all the specific prayers I had for myself and my friends and family. I made it through half of my list and felt a huge gust of a breeze brushing through the trees and so I got up and stood at the edge of the dock to take it in. And then I felt like God said to me, "Don't wait on the opportunity to be loved. Don't miss it."

I was startled. I had only heard God so clearly like that one other time. And what did God mean? In what way should I not wait for the opportunity to be loved? In friendships? In relationships? With Jesus? What could I potentially miss?

I sat back down and turned on a playlist of Today's Top Christian Hits on Spotify and hit shuffle to journal after hearing God, and the first song that came on was one I had never heard before called "I Don't Want To Miss It" by Ellie Holcomb.

I immediately burst into tears. "Hello, God?! What is going on?"

I couldn't believe the ways the Lord was trying to get my attention. Had He been trying to get my attention for some time, but I hadn't been still enough to hear what He was trying to say to me? As silly as it felt and sounded, this song randomly playing was a further affirmation that I had clearly heard what God was saying to me.

That day at Radnor Lake changed something in me. I still struggle with prayer and getting still enough to listen, but after sitting on the water with God, I realized He is listening and He wants to speak to me, I just need to be still.

I love meeting new people. If anyone figures out a way that I can easily meet 20 new people a day, I want to do that. The problem is, if I only hear their name once, there is not a single chance I will remember it. Every time I meet someone, I am so hyper-focused on what I am going to say next once they introduce themselves that I tend to miss out on what they say their name is. Granted, 95% of the time, I am gearing up to explain that no, my name is not

Mary. Yes, Mary Spencer is a double name. No, Spencer is not my last name or my maiden name.

I'm not always a good listener. These new friends end up repeating themselves because I missed what they said while I was focused on myself.

God has to repeat Himself often with me too, unfortunately. He's introducing Himself to me daily, but I'm already thinking about the next thing I need to do or say while He's speaking, missing out on what He's trying to show me.

Years ago, I was gifted the book *The Art of Listening Prayer* by Seth Barnes. I wanted to start having conversations that weren't so one-sided with God. I did not want to constantly ask, ask, ask, and not listen at all. As I read through the book, I began to recognize that I had overcomplicated prayer. I just needed to spend some time in Scripture asking the Lord to speak through His words to me, write down questions for prayer, and then pause, wait, and listen.

I really, truly try my hardest to listen. Seth Barnes says that the important thing is that you are allowing God to speak to you.[2] It does not matter where each of us is in our faith, from a brand new Christian to having known the Lord for decades, we all can talk to God. We don't have a magic formula for talking to Him. A million words do not have to be said. He wants to hear what we're hoping for, what we need forgiveness for, and then He wants us to just listen.

A new rhythm of mine I'm trying to incorporate into my every day is to put away all distractions, set a timer for 15 minutes, sit on my cream-colored comfy couch, and just pray. It's a small step, but it's changing something in my heart. Prayer reminds me that my life is not a coincidence. As I feel Him nudge me toward answers to my prayers, I know He is listening. When I give thanks for all that He's doing in my life, for all of the people He has brought into my life, my heart feels overwhelmed with gratitude in a way I don't experience outside of prayer. Prayer shifts my heart from all of my self-centered ways to a heart that knows Him more fully and is better for it.

As I've gotten older, I feel the freedom to pray at any time. I don't have to be in a certain place to pray. I can pray in my car or on a walk or sitting in a coffee shop. I can pray by reading over my wall of colorful sticky notes, recounting each prayer that I pray will be answered, and also reminding myself of each prayer that has already been answered. I feel Him listening and I see Him answering even over the smallest, silliest things. He is aware of my hopes and needs and knows before I ask, yet He still wants to hear from me. It is an honor to pray to the Creator of my soul, and I'm grateful He's listening.

I'll pray like my grandmothers do and did and will until their final breath: with hope, with love, and with adoration for our Creator, not overcomplicating it. Breathing in the simplicity of a conversation with our Father, hoping I one day too, can be a grandmother full of prayer for the ones she loves the most.

Chapter 4

INVEST IN A LOCAL CHURCH

As a girl from a small town who went to the same Baptist church for the first 18 years of her life, I did not know how in the world I would decide where to go to church when I moved to Nashville. Music City takes the phrase "a church on every corner" to a new level. I think we have something like 600+ churches in our community!

So instead of trying a million different churches, I jumped in with the first church I visited. It was a massive megachurch, and I fell in love with the worship and all the incredible pastors I got to hear from. I worked hard to meet people there and joined a small group (that wasn't so small, it had about seventy-five people in it) and started serving on the welcome team. I slowly started meeting people, but I still felt disconnected from the community since it was such a big church.

After about six months of living in Nashville, the pandemic hit, so church took place online. I'm so grateful for the way my church provided an online space each week for me and my family to learn and worship amid so much uncertainty. It was exactly what I needed during the few years of ups and downs of us all trying to return to in-person church.

When, slowly, we were allowed to go back to in-person church, I decided I wanted to try out other churches. The pandemic had shifted some of my priorities. My church was a good one and one that I'll always respect, but I now really desired to be a part of a smaller church where I could connect and see familiar faces each week.

I tried out just about every single church in Nashville to the point where I was overwhelmed. How would I ever decide? I had grown up in the same denomination my whole life, but I was at a point where I wasn't sure if I had a certain preference for the denomination, which made it hard to narrow down. What did I actually believe for myself? What did I value? I finally landed on a church for a short period and started attending on Sundays but struggled to meet people my own age. It was full of families but very few single 20-somethings and was still a lot bigger than I hoped for.

In an attempt to "branch out," I had refrained from going to the church a lot of my friends went to. I wanted to meet new people and do something different, but after a lot of life changes, I found myself sitting in the black fold-out chairs of the church that my friends attended on a Sunday morning in February 2023.

I immediately connected with the preaching at this church. I loved the wide variety of ages I saw as I looked around. I could see how much this church cared about getting Young Professionals plugged into the local church and caring for them as much as any other age demographic. This church was five minutes from my house too, and I thought it'd be nice to go to a church that was in my neighborhood.

So I committed at that moment that this would be my church, and I would walk through its red doors every single Sunday that I was in town. I would quit looking for flaws… although I will say I'm hoping one day there is a golf cart to escort me from the place I have to park six blocks away if I come to the 11 o'clock service.

I knew this church preached the Gospel each week, and I felt a peace that I had been yearning for all along. I immediately signed up for a Young Professionals girls' Bible Study and started attending a church service every Sunday I was in town. I felt right at home and decided I needed to really commit. I needed to become a member and truly invest in this church. No more hopping around. No more hiding in the shadows on Sundays sneaking in and out of church and letting that be it. I needed more, and God was asking for more of me too.

Church being so readily available on the Internet is an incredible thing, and I am so grateful that churches can livestream and record. But I don't know if it's healthy for us to lean on watching from home as our crutch and the only way we participate in church. Of course, there are exceptions to the rule– if you are physically unable to get to church or dealing with a sickness that prevents you from going in public spaces–but if you can access a church and be in person it will serve your soul in ways that being online cannot feed.

Being a part of a local church not only on Sundays but also by joining a community group and volunteering are ways to invest in our relationship with Jesus and build a family within a space of believers. These people will hopefully encourage, challenge, and pour into you and me.

My friend Shelly is someone who has invested in the life of her church, and the blessings from her investment multiply every time I see her. She shows up at church. She has built true, deep relationships with the people within her church. She cares for the members of her church and is giving back to her community.

Recently, Shelly had a surgery that she was going to need to spend a few weeks recovering from. She had been laid off from her job a couple of weeks prior, but Shelly was not stressed about how she would make ends meet. Sure, she was being proactive and looking for a job and preparing for her surgery, but she was not letting this cripple her daily walk with Jesus.

I sat with her a week before her surgery, and she was talking through what the procedure would be like and wondering how she was going to pay rent. As we sat there, her phone rang and she put it on speaker. A woman from her church was calling. It was the end of the month, and the woman told Shelly she realized she had a little money left over from her monthly budget and wanted to send Shelly some money to pay for groceries and bills. Shelly had mentioned she had been laid off from her job to her friend weeks ago but had no idea what way this woman was going to bless her. I was almost as moved as Shelly was.

The next week after Shelly's surgery, Shelly's church family showed up daily, if not hourly, with baked goods, groceries, meals, everything she could possibly need. She had countertops decorated with a variety of sweet treats and a fridge stuffed with home-cooked meals. She couldn't eat it all and was begging people to come and take food off of her hands.

I was blown away by how Shelly's church family showed up for her in a time of need, but the beautiful part is I know Shelly would and has done the same for others when they have needs. Shelly's first question to me every time I call her is, "How are you doing, really? What's going on, what do you need?"

I'm lucky to have her as a friend, and she has been such an example to me of what it means to invest in your church family and show up time and time again. I asked Shelly why she thinks it's important to invest in the local church and what she said is so beautiful: "You look outside of all the craziness and there are these people that come together every single week, looking for hope. You have access to people with the same mindset, and so I know investing in the church is important. You've joined a powerful team!"

I am trying my hardest to be like Shelly, fully committing to a church and planting roots. I want people around me who are like-minded in their faith and will hold me accountable and show me love all in the same breath. A verse I am reminded of when I think about the importance of investing in a church family is Matthew 18:20: *"For where two or three are gathered in my name, there am I among them."* We are better together and are sharpened by other believers spurring us on in our faith.

It's hard to see much good that came from the isolation of the pandemic, but one thing became blatantly clear to me during that time: we need each other. Not just on Facetime or Zoom calls, while that can be good and serve a purpose. We need relationships that are built together by being in the same room. We need to gather together.

At the beginning of the Bible, God says, *"It is not good that the man should be alone; I will make him a helper fit for him"* (Genesis 2:18). Life alone is not the life we are created for. Many times throughout Scripture, Christians are referred to as sheep and the Lord as our shepherd. Sheep are not the smartest animals in the world. They need direction.

Sheep are safer together. When they are left unprotected, alone, and vulnerable, sheep are at risk of being injured, lost, or killed. We need protection, accountability, and guidance from those around us and most importantly from our Shepherd.

Joining a church is also a ball of fun. As I'm writing this, I'm in the process of joining my church in Nashville. At our first membership class, I was able to connect with other potential members, learn more about the church's beliefs, and meet some of the church leadership.

Here's what I know: Joining a church is fun, but staying in a church is the hard part. You will not agree with everything that happens at church. You may not agree with every single belief that church leadership holds. The people inside the church will fail you at times because sinful humans make up churches.

But does the church believe that Jesus dying on the Cross for our sins provides us with grace to be connected and unified with God if we have faith and believe? If so, the next thing you will have to determine is what your preferences are. Do you want to belong to a certain denomination? Do you want a twelve-piece worship band or would you rather have a few people strumming guitars and singing old hymns? Do you want a traditional or contemporary setting?

What should we be looking for in a church when we're on the hunt for a place to commit to? Deciding what's important for you when it comes to a church is a huge and important step in your faith because a church family helps shape your faith and come alongside you to help you grow in kingdom work.

Here's a list of a few questions that really mattered to me when deciding what church I'd attend:

1. DO THEY PREACH THE GOSPEL?

Between my old job and an interest in seeing how all different churches operate, I have been to just about every kind of church you can imagine. I have noticed we have some churches that are preaching feel-good messages while others are preaching from the Word of God. I have a feeling you will be able to sense in your spirit which of the two a church you visit falls into.

This is the most important part of determining what church is right for you. With so many options for churches, especially if you are like me and live in a big city in the South, you are probably able to try out enough churches to last you through the year. My encouragement would be to do your research on churches in your area, make a list of your top five or so, and make a plan to visit each of them. Get a sense of how they do church and community.

In the Christian world, there are also numerous denominations. I grew up Baptist, and then when I went off to college I was a part of a Baptist church for three years before switching to a nondenominational church. I then attended a nondenominational church for the first few years in Nashville before finally landing in a Presbyterian church. (I hope you find the right church family a lot quicker than I did!)

I have done tons of research into a lot of the different denominations to figure out what I agree with and disagree with. I don't believe there is the perfect denomination that has it all right or that I will agree and align perfectly with and that's okay. I see moments and arguments between various denominations when we need to align for a common cause: sharing and spreading the Gospel. It's okay to have different views, but when we hone in on what makes us different instead of what unifies us we then lose sight of what the Gospel really is. I spent a lot of time caught up in trying to find the perfect church and the perfect denomination and after way too much time it's hit me that there is no right answer. Jump in somewhere after doing your research and be all in.

2. HOW DOES CHURCH LEADERSHIP CARE FOR THE CHURCH FAMILY?

In what ways do they disciple their members? Do they have community groups? How do they care for their congregation and what is their priority for their members? Hopefully, in all that they do, they will be pointing you and me back to the cross and helping lead people to Jesus who have not yet experienced Him and His love. As I've been a part of several different churches throughout the past decade, I've seen churches that do this well and some that don't.

What I'm looking for in church leaders are people who show humility, are approachable, display empathy while also holding those around them accountable, and are willing to be held accountable as well. I also am always interested in how the church spends its money and what is built into its budget.

Working for a church is a hard, difficult job. Every mistake is magnified, and I know it can be a thankless job. I'm so grateful for those who have stepped into church leadership roles, I seriously am. But as a church leader, I do have hopes for how they will care for their congregation and am looking for those qualities in the church leaders before committing to a church.

3. WHAT DOES THE CHURCH FAMILY LOOK LIKE?

Are there all different ages, stages, and people in all sorts of walks of life attending this church? I don't want everyone to be the same, look the same, or act the same as me. I want older church members to learn from. I want a joyful chaos of kids running around me at church, crawling, walking, running, hopping along in all of life's ages and stages.

Nashville is a city where thousands of twenty-somethings run to immediately after they move the tassel on their graduation cap from right to left. After the first few weeks of May, Nashville has an explosion of 22-year-olds becoming residents of our city. I was once one of them. This city is filled with a gazillion twenty-somethings and so our churches tend to be too. I love having so many people my age in my city, but I wanted to find a church that had a wide variety of ages too.

I want a kaleidoscope of a church family. I want to look around and feel like I'm at a potluck of personalities that shouldn't make sense when combined together but somehow they just do. We are sharpened by those older than us, from different backgrounds as us, and are in different seasons of life than us. We have so much to learn from each other.

Then, all the other hopes for a church will fall into place. Maybe I give up what I hope worship will look like for the sake of having a church family that leads well and preaches the Gospel. All outside of that is just a bonus. I'm thankful to live in a place where I can easily access a church and live in a community with my brothers and sisters in Christ. What a gift that is.

Chapter 5

THE POWER OF
MENTORSHIP

When I started graduate school at Belmont, I was told that I could sign up to receive a faith mentor. I was thrilled because I craved having an older, wiser voice in my life, especially now that I had once again moved to a new, unfamiliar city. I filled out the form about the kind of mentor I was looking for: someone who worked for a ministry or nonprofit who could share their experiences with me and help me navigate what direction I wanted to go in for a career.

A few weeks later a notification lit up in my email inbox saying I had finally been paired with a mentor! I couldn't open the email fast enough; it felt like Christmas.

My mentor would be, drum roll please… a man who was retiring from accounting?

Now listen, I was open to the possibilities, but I wasn't really looking for a male mentor. I also have nothing against an accountant, some of my very best friends are accountants. But I have zero, none, zilch interest in accounting. I responded back and asked if they happened to have any female mentors. They told me they'd see what they could do, but at the moment they did not have any female mentors.

I figured all hope was lost on being paired with a mentor. How hard was it to find a woman to mentor me? It was worth a try, I thought, but I would need to find someone through a different avenue.

Months later, someone I loved dearly was considering going to treatment for an addiction they were battling. I was full of hope that this could be a turning point in their life, but then a few days before they were supposed to go to treatment, they backed out. It had been years in the making trying to get this person to go to treatment, and I felt like we finally had hope. I was crushed.

The very same week my friend backed out of going to treatment, I got an email saying I had been paired with a new mentor. I had kind of forgotten about it at this point because it had been a while, but I clicked on the email to see who they had now found for me.

Her name was Kate and she worked for a faith-based nonprofit called The Next Door. Check and check! I was ecstatic. I Googled The Next Door to see what kind of work they do… and it turned out that they are an addiction treatment center for women.

I was a little bit stunned. What were the odds, Lord? I emailed Kate right away asking when we could meet. She sent me a date and time to come visit her at work, and I counted down the days until I could meet her face-to-face and see this place.

Driving over to The Next Door for the very first time, I told myself that I would not tell Kate about this friend of mine who was struggling with an addiction. It wasn't something I ever talked about with anyone. Addiction seemed like this big, hairy monster that we weren't supposed to talk about.

I walked up to the front door, rang the doorbell, and held my breath as I waited for the front office to let me in. I was immediately blown away by what I saw. I walked through the same front door that each woman walked through to come to treatment. I saw women who were battling an addiction treated as equals, and it deeply moved me.

A beautiful, bubbly blonde woman walked up to me, hugged me, and introduced herself as Kate. She took me up to her office where her German Shorthaired Pointer, Archie, greeted me. We sat down in Kate's office, and she asked me lots of deep, personal questions. I broke down five minutes into meeting her. I told her all about my friend and what was going on. Just seeing what treatment could be like for my friend pained me because I didn't know if they would ever make it to a place like this.

And so began our friendship. I'm surprised she didn't ghost me after a stranger like me cried in her office upon our first meeting. Turns out that's the kind of effect Kate has on a person, she makes each person she encounters feel like an old friend and someone you can trust. Kate and I would meet once a month after that and catch up. She would give me advice and listen to what was happening in my life.

Eventually, I became a volunteer at The Next Door helping write grants and other miscellaneous tasks needed in the development department. Kate told me that I would work for a nonprofit one day, and I laughed. I was getting my MBA and had no interest in being employed in the nonprofit sphere.

Turns out Kate can see the future too. But we'll get there.

I was then introduced to Masi. My mom and Masi had grown up together, and Masi had moved to Nashville shortly before me. She saw my Mom's Facebook post saying that I had just moved to Nashville and reached out to say if I ever wanted someone to hang out with, she'd love to meet me! The not-so-shy person that I am, I took her up on her offer. We started meeting regularly too. Masi showed me all sorts of spots around Franklin and Leiper's Fork and made me feel right at home in a place where my family was seven hours away. We talked about beginning again in a big city when we grew up in such small ones, dating, and our wild ideas for the future.

I've always been hesitant toward any formal, rigid businessy buzzwords. Networking? No. Mentors? What does that even mean? A lot of times I felt like people were trying to acquire mentors that would help them climb the corporate ladder, and I wasn't exactly interested in that.

I was looking for some friends a few decades ahead of me who could walk me through where they'd already been. I kept showing up at the doors God put right in front of my face. He softball tossed these people to me, and I was going to be an idiot if I missed out on them.

A few years after meeting both of these incredible mentors of mine, I started my first job and had to plan a fundraising event for 600+ people. One of the chairs for the event was a gorgeous, hilarious woman named Caroline. In her forties, she had four children, about as many dogs, and had a lot of the same dreams as me. We spent a lot of time together planning our big event, and when it was over, we remained close friends. She became a mentor to me in so many ways.

She saw me through the beginning, middle, and end of a relationship and called to give me advice all along the way. She also saw me through the beginning, middle, and end of my first job and helped me think through what would be next in a season that felt like a lot of endings. She wrote and published a book right before I landed my book deal and gave me her best advice through all of this too.

I have a handful of women in my life that I consider mentors now and these three have impacted my life in ways I'll never be able to put into words or give enough gratitude to. I didn't have to search far to find them, but I did have to actively seek them out. Every opportunity I've had in Nashville I owe to each of them. They opened doors for me that I couldn't have opened for myself. I am so utterly grateful for the way they have carried me when I didn't know if I could make it to the next starting line.

A friend asked me the other day, "How do you find all of these mentors? I want one!"

I had wondered the very same thing while I was in college. I had heard professors and friends talk about mentors, but they always seemed like these mystical people that I had to awkwardly ask to take me under their wing. It doesn't have to be that way, though. I guess it could be, but as someone who hates the term "networking" and doesn't want to burden anyone, that's not the way I approach it at all.

Mentors are people who naturally gel as puzzle pieces in your life. They have interests and passions that align with yours, but they may have more life experience than you, giving you a new perspective. They've walked the roads you may be seeking to travel down. It's a two-way relationship, though. You don't just take, take, take from a mentor. You provide encouragement and support to them too, just maybe in different ways.

Who do you have in your life that could be a mentor to you? Maybe it's an acquaintance you met at a work event or an older woman in your church. Think about someone you'd love to spend more time with and learn from. Ask them to get coffee or go on a walk around their neighborhood.

When I moved to Nashville, it was such a blessing having some older women in my life since I had no family in town and was only spending time with people my age. I craved spending time with people of all ages, women that I could learn from and that could challenge me.

My list of women I consider mentors continues to grow. Some I see often, but most of them I see once a month or maybe every other month. I am always grateful for any time spent with them.

Throughout my twenties, relationships have formed, stopped, grown, died, and a little bit of everything in between. They have breathed in and out, fluctuating in a way I did not know to expect. Without the guidance of my mentors, I don't know if I would have been able to discern what and who I should let go of versus what and who to fight for. I need their persistence and check-ins as I make sense of the growing pains happening in this decade of my life. I am indebted to these women for making a little room for me in their busy, full lives. I love more deeply; I fight for what I want more courageously and I know Jesus more fully because of the ways they have cared for me.

Spoiler alert: Kate was right and now I have worked in the nonprofit world for years. Each nonprofit I have been a part of has a Board of Directors. These men and women come from all different backgrounds and walks of life. Some are lawyers, others are real estate agents. We have full-time moms and full-time professors. Having a variety of professions and personalities makes our board strong. What we are looking for in board members, though, are people who want to uplift our nonprofit's mission, who believe in what we're doing wholeheartedly, and who will bring light and resources to further our mission. We need a team outside of the team we already have.

What is so special to me about a Board of Directors is that they have nothing to gain. They aren't paid employees; they are people who love and care about serving their community through a very specific organization.

As I've watched and become friends with all sorts of people through the different boards I've known through my work, I have begun to recognize the need for a personal and professional board in my own life.

What I see is this: we all have and need boards in our lives, our own personal and professional Board of Directors. We need people to guide, lead, and accompany us as we walk through life in our careers and in our community outside of work. What does it look like to have a Board of Directors for your life?

Mentors fill gaps I cannot fill for myself. They have connections and callings that I do not have. I admire them and want to shape my life in a similar way to how they are shaping their own lives. My mentors who serve as a part of my Board of Directors have lived more life than me and as believers, they also point me back to the Cross when my compass starts pointing any other direction but North.

They are my friends, but they are also the ones setting me up for success and guiding my hands along the monkey bars as I swing along, not sure if my grip can continue to hold me up.

But we keep swinging on and on. They will tell me when it is time to drop down and switch to a new path. I trust them because I have seen the way the Lord has worked in each of their lives and careers and we have lived enough life together at this point that each of them knows my heart and my dreams and desires.

We are better together. Intertwining our lives with so many people lifts us up and leads us home. Mentors give us the space to learn who we are through the example they provide by inviting us into their lives. I am who I am because of these women who paved the path before me. They reach behind to lift each of us up with hopes that we will one day do the same for those coming up behind us. I hope to be more like them.

Chapter 6

SABBATH - A GIFT FOR YOUR SOUL

J ust about every Sunday, I begin well-intentioned. I want to have a true day of rest, but I don't know how to slow down. I want to cram a million activities in one day. I start off my Sundays thinking I won't get on social media, I especially won't waste my time on TikTok.... I want so badly to rest. I want my mind to have a moment to breathe before starting the week again. But then I find myself scrolling Sunday afternoon and wasting all the time in the world. I have a hard time writing this chapter because I'm not sure if there is anything more that I struggle with than having a true day of rest. How do I get myself to do this?

Annie F. Downs, a favorite author and speaker of mine, once said something that stuck with me: "If you work with your mind, Sabbath with your hands. If you work with your hands, Sabbath with your mind."[3] I spend the majority of my time on my computer fundraising for the nonprofit I work for, so I need to Sabbath with my hands. In my tiny apartment, there isn't a lot of room for activities, so I am having to get creative on Sabbathing with my hands. I would love to be a puzzle kind of girl, but if I get stumped for too long, I become irritated and intolerable.

Maybe that means that I actually do need to become a puzzle person, but for now, I'll pass.

Moving my body on Sabbath helps. Being outdoors and walking is restful for me, especially when I leave the AirPods behind and just enjoy nature for what it is instead of filling my mind with music or a podcast.

Jesus tells us, "Come to me, all who labor and are heavy laden, and I will give you rest. Take my yoke upon you, and learn from me, for I am gentle and lowly in heart, and you will find rest for your souls. For my yoke is easy, and my burden is light."

My heart and hands are heavy, yet I find myself trying to carry my load alone. I don't want to fall behind, and it feels wasteful to move so slowly on my day of rest, but that's my problem. If I can't quiet my mind, I can't quiet my heart. And if I can't quiet my heart, then I become out of rhythm with Jesus. I want to walk in step with Him, but I can't hear where He's going or what He's saying with so many distractions. So how do we make rest happen when it doesn't come naturally for our souls to do so?

Rest will not happen without intention. We need to schedule time for rest. So here's my plan on how I can be sure to follow through each week on making it a practice to have a true Sabbath:

1. **Determine what day will be best for your day of rest at the beginning of the week.** Most people will probably choose Sundays as their day of rest, but Sundays might not always be possible for you. Maybe you're a nurse and you work on Sundays, or you're going on a trip with friends and can't make Sunday work. That's okay! Evaluate at the beginning of the week which day will work best for you.

2. **Have accountability for your day of rest.** Tell your friends what day you'll be resting and what you're planning to do for your day of rest. Having someone aware of your plan for rest makes it a lot more likely that you will carry it out.

3. **Ditch the phone.** If you're like me and have a hard time staying off social media for a whole day (seriously, why do I lack so much self-control?), consider putting your phone up for the day or deleting social media apps from your phone. For so long, I've tried to use Screen Time on my phone to keep me accountable, but I'm quick to press ignore when I've passed my allotted amount of time. Throw your phone in a drawer or leave it in your car and unplug it. I'm trying to implement a new strategy of spending less time on my phone in general by attempting the 1 month, 1 week, 1-day rule where you delete social media for 1 month per year, 1 week per month, and 1 day per week.

I feel like a better version of myself when I spend less time seeing every single moment of everyone else's lives. Resting and mindlessly scrolling do not go hand in hand as much as we want them to. Studies show that doom scrolling leads to a dependence on dopamine, leading our minds to rely on receiving it over and over from moving quickly through as many social media posts as we can.[4] We need to find rest without reliance on a screen. Our minds are begging us to detox from our dependence on our phones.

4. **Plan some fun.** Later in the book, we will talk about hobbies, and days of rest are the perfect time to engage in the hobbies you have. Read, write, walk, paint, and work on a puzzle. Collect rocks or stamps if that's your cup of tea. As our dear friend the Cat in the Hat said, "It's fun to have fun, but you have to know how."[5] Fun does not come naturally, especially as we get older and the weight of the world wraps its arms around us.

Here are some ideas for your day of rest (and feel free to add to the list!)

▸ Make a cup of tea and read a book on your porch

▸ Write a letter to your best friend

▸ Walk around your local park soaking up the sunshine

▸ Take a nap (as someone who takes naps maybe twice a year, I envy those of you who can nap easily)

▸ Read a new Bible study and spend some time with Jesus

▸ Go to a yoga class

▸ Invite a friend over to work on a puzzle with you (because I'm certainly not doing that alone)

▸ Try something new like taking up flower pressing or rock climbing or learning how to build a rocket

And here's what you don't have to feel obligated to do on your day of rest (I'm talking to myself especially):

▸ Unloading the dishwasher

▸ Doing laundry

▸ Catching up on a few work emails

▸ Scrolling through social media for an hour

▸ Taking out the trash

▸ Running errands

I'm embarrassed to say today is Sunday and I've already done half of the things on this list. I've gotten my groceries, taken out the trash, and rested very little. I'm not going to beat myself up about it, but I am going to try to figure out how to get more of these chores done before Sunday comes so I can truly rest. I need to invite people into my day of rest, holding me accountable to truly take this gift for my soul.

I'm tired. Really, really tired. Working all week, then spending time writing, hanging with friends, and doing the very basic tasks I need to do each day has left me drained. I need this day of rest each week desperately.

I'm betting you do too, friend. The Sleep Center of Middle Tennessee has an article titled, "Millennials: The Tired Generation." In this article, they discuss why millennials are so tired: financial and career challenges, poor diet and exercise, and too much time spent on our phones are all contributing factors.[6] Having Sunday as a reset can help us reevaluate if we are taking care of ourselves throughout the whole week, not just on Sunday.

———

One of my favorite restaurants in Nashville is a sushi place called Virago. It's easy to miss if you are just passing by on the street or not sure what you are looking for. Virago's black wooden doors are nestled in between an outdoor hallway of sorts flanked by two other restaurants. Walking in feels like an elevated experience: everyone is enamored in conversation and melting into their seats with each savory bite of sushi.

I typically start my nights at Virago with a Wasabi Martini, followed by Crispy Rice and Spicy Tuna sprinkled with watermelon pop rocks detonating in my mouth. My roll of choice always and forever will be the Truffle Futomaki: an explosion of flavors featuring panko shrimp, pickled ginger, jalapeños, scallions, avocados, albacore, yuzu truffle, cilantro, unagi sauce, and red tobiko. Now I'm hungry.

If I ever win the lottery, I'm confident of two things: I will have a chauffeur because I would prefer to never drive myself anywhere ever again, and I will have Virago at least 3 times a week.

Savoring each bite of a meal brings a new appreciation for the experience in front of me, especially when I hold it up to other nights when I might be scrolling through my phone while eating a microwave meal from trusty Trader Joe's. A meal is a meal, but the experience is different.

I tend to microwave my faith and my Sundays. It tastes okay, but I know it could be different. I know what it's like to have faith like those watermelon pop rocks detonating in my mouth, full of wonder and an explosion of joy. I have tasted and seen that the Lord is good, yet I rarely slow down long enough to savor what He's gifted me with. I want a crockpot kind of faith, one that develops over time and isn't rushed or hurried, enjoying every moment and minute that passes.

Last night after work, I began my drive to the lake for Labor Day weekend. I had a 7-hour drive ahead of me, but I broke up my trip and stopped in Atlanta last night to visit my best friend Savannah's new place.

When I rush to the next destination over and over, I miss the savoring. Stopping and grabbing dinner with my friend who knows me like few people do filled my cup up in a way that will carry me through the week.

As I continued on my drive, I stopped after a few hours in Perry, Georgia, a small, vibrant town nestled in the middle of the state, to get some coffee and lunch. It was a strange experience, not rushing to get where I was going. I savored every moment and every bite.

Then, my mom called me. "Want to meet me for a pedicure in Tifton?" I responded with, "No, I don't feel like adding an extra hour to my ETA," but as I hung up the phone, I felt a tug. Slow down. Savor. So I packed up my bag and went out of my way just a little to spend some extra moments with my mom, and as a bonus, I now have nails the color of blueberry milk.

I feel my body exhaling. Not always operating on my timeline and holding my plans loosely leaves a gap that can be filled in ways that I'm better for. Unexpected conversations and moments that I wouldn't have if I was always operating on my agenda.

A mindset that seeks rest allows space to slow down and savor. Agendas leave us longing for more, but spaces for God give us hope in unexpected, small ways. Pastor and author of *Core 52* Mark E. Moore once said, "When the rhythm of rest punctuates our work, we'll experience more productivity at work and more connectivity at home. This is the life God wants for you as much as you do."[7]

Rest is a gift to us from God. We weren't made for rest; rest was made *for* us. God knew giving it our all six days a week would be challenging and exhausting, and recharging our batteries would be necessary to fill up our cups. It's a gift we feel guilty using because what if we get behind or miss out?

But what if we miss out on the gift? What if we never know what could lie ahead for us because we are too busy rushing trying to catch up? What or who are we even trying to "catch up" to? God is inviting us to slow down enough to remember who we are and what we are. It's hard to drown out the noise when we never stop moving.

We need Sabbath. It's a gift, freely given, that helps us become better, more whole humans. I want to take God up on the treasure of living a little slower, just for one day.

I moved to Nashville 4 years ago, and I've lived in 4 different houses. The first house was on the sweetest street where I shared a bathroom with three girls (how did we do that?), but after our ceiling collapsed in our kitchen one night (more on that later), we decided it might be time to move on to a new place. I then moved into a fun, three-story townhouse with two friends, but after we kept having attempted break-ins to our house and cars, we decided we needed to move. By the third move, I had it in my mind that I didn't need to get comfortable anywhere for too long. Another move could be imminent at any moment. After a year in an apartment with my best friend, I decided to move into a one-bedroom.

It was my first space that was truly all mine. It was no longer a joint decision on how long I'd stay here. No one had input on what furniture I had in the living room, what decor to set up throughout the place, or who got what corner of the apartment. I was calling the shots.

I don't know how long I'll stay, but for once, I want to set up like I'll be here for a long time. I want to feel at home. I need that after such a crazy year. I crave a safe space that I can come home to every day.

I quickly realized how little furniture I owned. I needed a lot: a couch, a TV stand, a rug, a coffee table, patio furniture, the list goes on. Now, I wasn't so certain I wanted to call the shots. The shots were getting expensive, and there seemed to be only a zillion different options for every little thing I needed.

I'm sitting here in my little nook of the world after putting it all together, and I'm so proud of the space that

I've designed. It's my own. It looks like me. It feels like me. I feel at ease here. I feel safe.

I've been anxious to get every little thing for my apartment: the decor and tables and the twinkly lights and pillows, but as I look around now all settled in my new home, I feel like I'm also finally settling into this city I've called my home for four years. I'm not waiting for the next move, the next moment. Part of me will always want to rush to the next chapter of life, but I feel myself slowing down and enjoying this place God has called me to. I don't know how long I'll be here, with these people, in this city, but I'm grateful He's led me here.

We get to cast our anxieties on Him as He cares for us. Our lives were never meant to be this overloaded, this full, to the point where we feel like we'll never catch up. Slowing down invites God in. It's a whole lot easier for me to hear Jesus when I'm not running a marathon in my mind and in my world every single day.

I love what theologian Eugene Peterson says about the Sabbath, "If you don't take a Sabbath, something is wrong. You're doing too much, you're being too much in charge. You've got to quit, one day a week, and just watch what God is doing when you're not doing anything."[8] I want my whole life to feel like one long Sabbath. Unrushed, unhurried, unbothered by the past, and unconcerned with what's to come. Space to breathe brings to life creativity in me. When I'm smothered with work and running around trying to meet every need, I neglect the need inside of me to care for myself in restful and creative ways.

With rest and rhythms of a slower life, I feel a nudge to speed up to the world's pace. But as I become more in tune with *who* I am, I then begin to see my soul untangle from the world's expectations and settle into what Jesus has for me.

It's not easy and it's not natural, but this slower pace of life feeds my soul in a way the world never could. Sabbath is a practice my soul certainly needs and slowness is a gift that keeps on giving. Let it keep breathing life into you and me as we begin to roll back who we are, one layer at a time.

Crossroad 2

WHO YOU ARE

On a friend's bachelorette trip, we drove over to this old, quaint schoolhouse in Nashville. The building had been a school in the 1930s but had been since converted into a restaurant and event space. Upon arrival, we were led down the steps to a basement and I began to grow concerned. Where were we going?

What met us below was a room with pottery lining the walls in an array of colors and shapes. We sat down to our very own blob of beige clay. It held no particular shape; it just existed with hopes to be something more.

As I ran my hands around the clay, it began to take shape. At first, it looked like a bowl. Then, it began to look like the world's smallest vase. I guided it along, trying to decide what I hoped the final product would be.

We are all being shaped and molded by something or someone every day. In a world where you can be anything and everything, I wanted to begin the book by laying the foundation of *whose* we are. Whether you are Jewish, Muslim, atheist, or Christian, your identity is rooted in someone or something. It's up to you to decide *whose* you will be, and that will bring clarity to *who* you will become.

We come into this world like that lump of clay. We were designed by a Creator who wants to shape us further into who He is calling us to be. We will be shaped into lots of different versions of ourselves throughout our lives.

This past year felt like I was twisted into a pretzel, but I am slowly being unwinded into something new, and for that, I am grateful.

This second section is all about the struggle and joy that comes with discerning who we are, especially in our 20s. It's a wild decade of life. It's hard; it's good; it's holy, and it's here. Thank you for being here, friend.

Chapter 7

BODY AS A TEMPLE – PHYSICALLY AND EMOTIONALLY

stopped weighing myself when I was 21 years old. For the better part of a decade, I beat myself up and obsessed over three little numbers I would see on a scale. I'd eat healthy, and work out consistently, and the number would go up, or it would barely change. Defeated, I would stare at myself in the mirror, trying to will my stomach into being flatter. That's the only thing I cared about.

Eventually, I got sick of obsessing over a number, and I refused to know my weight. In the doctor's office? Sure, you can weigh me but do not tell me what it says. I don't care anymore.

The summer after I graduated from college, I stayed and worked in Auburn and spent all the time in the world with my friends. We spent most days at our friend's apartment pool or the lake or basically any place that had some form of water readily available for us to jump in, cooling off from the Alabama summer heat.

One weekend, we were at a friend's lake house swimming, jumping, and running in and out of that lake all day. The girls I hung out with that summer, old friends and some new, were the absolute most fun. I can't remember a time when I had more fun than I did that summer.

The only thing that was not perfect: I felt a little insecure every time I was in a bathing suit around them. I have a perfectly good body size and type, but here I was surrounded by six-pack abs. I felt like a garden gnome among Greek goddesses.

As we sat around at the lake that weekend, a guy friend of mine said, "You've got an athletic build, don't you?"

I don't remember why this came up in conversation. Some people may have been offended by this comment, but I wasn't in the slightest. Why yes, friend. I've got an athletic build. He said it like it was just a fact. It wasn't a compliment or insult, and I was grateful he made it sound like it was a very casual matter and not something to be thought of twice.

Such a silly, insignificant moment that I bet my friend doesn't even remember, but something in my brain switched that day into respecting my body a little bit more. My body was athletic and good and that was that.

———

I have tried about every type of workout class in the world: barre, cycling, yoga, HIIT, and everything in between. When the pandemic happened, I was on a big boxing kick, but I had to go from dodging punches to dodging people's germs… ending my short-lived boxing endeavors.

I hadn't ever been a big yoga girl, too slow of a pace for me, but I decided to get a two week pass to a yoga studio a few blocks from my house for a month since they were open during the pandemic. People who can balance on their heads intimidate me but my options were limited with all that was happening in the world, so I gave it a try.

I walked up the concrete steps to the yoga studio, went to my assigned spot, and rolled out my purple and gray mat. The walls were white with yellow paint spelling out the word "SHINE" across one side of the studio. The room smelled like lavender and the instructor's voice was soothing from her very first word.

I had no idea what to expect, and at first, I really struggled with the pace of yoga. It left me with too much room for my thoughts. Fast-paced cardio workouts didn't allow much thinking outside of trying to remember to breathe.

But now I was remembering to breathe differently. I felt like I learned something new about myself with every yoga class that I finished. I was stronger than I thought. My body was more beautiful and important than I had ever known.

Every time I entered a class, I looked around to find women and men of all different ages and sizes. Some people moved fast, some slow, and some not at all (child's pose for the win). I became a fan of who I was becoming because of my time spent on a purple and gray mat in this small yoga studio.

My great-great grandfather A.V. Kennedy lived to be 103 1/2 years old. Until the end of his life, he went for a walk after almost every meal. With or without you, company or no company, he was going. And he was going fast, he walked with purpose and you had to do all you could to keep up with him.

I don't know a lot of people who lived to 103, so great-great grandad A.V. might have been onto something. He got up, and moved his body every day, even when people would have been able to give him every excuse not to.

Moving my body daily keeps me sane. Intentional movement, whether that's yoga, walking, or lifting weights makes my muscles and mind feel sharp instead of sluggish. Our bodies were made to move. They were made to jump on trampolines and skate down sidewalks and run (or in my case walk) down neighborhood streets and through parks. I hear God better when I'm spending time each day moving my body.

The CDC even says that exercise combats health conditions and diseases, improves your mood, boosts energy, promotes better sleep, and encourages socializing when in a group setting.[9]

What's a form of exercise you enjoy? Are you an OrangeTheory or Barry's Bootcamp kind of gal? (If so, I envy you. Nothing sounds more like my worst nightmare than jogging on a treadmill with strangers in a class. I wish I wanted to.) Do you love to walk? Do you prefer to exercise alone or in a group?

I'll always choose a walk, well, except this week because it's 3 degrees in Nashville. This South Georgia girl is used to school being canceled if it got below 40 degrees because there was *potential* for ice on the ground.

I thrive being outside. The European Journal of Preventive Cardiology did a study that absolutely fascinated me. Their study suggested that for people under age 60, walking between 7,000 and 13,000 steps per day lowered the overall risk of death by 49%. For those ages 60 and older, walking 6,000 to 10,000 daily steps lowered the risk by 42%.[10] Not bad benefits for something free if I do say so myself.

I just have to think it matters to God that we take care of the bodies He's given us, but His love isn't conditional based on what we weigh, how much we exercise, what we eat, none of that. Health looks different for each person, so I can't compare myself to others. I'm grateful for the resources the Lord has provided that allow me to care for my body and mind like the gift that it is.

———

Growing up, I didn't really know anyone who went to counseling. I'm sure I had classmates that went to therapy, but I never knew if they did. It wasn't something that was talked about. As I went off to college, I had friends who more openly talked about counseling, but I still thought it was only for people who had experienced massive, traumatic events.

Once I got to Nashville, though, it seemed like a normal staple in the routines of the people around me. Lots of people were in counseling. I didn't understand it, and the thought of going to counseling honestly scared me.

What in the world would we talk about, and why should I go if I don't have any crazy big problems?

I had a friend eventually tell me that I should find a counselor. Confused, I asked her why and she told me that it's better to find someone before a crisis does occur because once those major life events come up, it's hard to find someone quickly... and counseling wasn't just for major life events either. News to me.

I finally decided to bite the bullet and try this counseling thing out. On a sweltering hot Tuesday in June, I did my intake for counseling over Zoom. The woman asked me some pretty standard questions, questions that I expected to be asked about why I wanted to find a counselor, and then it was over. I felt a little bit like crying after all of it because talking about my life somewhat personally with a stranger was disarming, but she was such a nice woman and assured me they'd find me a counselor in the next few months. I wasn't worried; I didn't think I had a huge need for it anyway.

The same night as my intake, I woke up to a loud noise. It was 3 am, and none of my roommates were in town. It sounded like someone was running up my stairs. In a panic, I jumped up, locked my bedroom door, ran into my bathroom, and called my boyfriend. I couldn't believe that he picked up, but I told him how scared I was, and he raced right over. He told me to call 911, but I couldn't do it. What if it was just all in my head?

He arrived in record time and called me to say it didn't look like anyone had broken in. He told me to come down the stairs and let him in. I was frozen in a state of shock, and it took me a while to come down those two flights of stairs. As soon as I let him in, I started sobbing uncontrollably.

No one was in the house. It was all in my head… well, maybe it was. We had had a lot of break-ins around our house during that summer, so my mind could've been playing tricks on me, but it was because these home invasions were happening in real life all around me.

I didn't sleep through the night for almost a year after that. I would wake up almost every night at 3 am in a panic that someone was breaking into our house. I slept with the door to my room locked. As someone who is usually pretty fearless, this newfound fear was taking a massive toll on me, mentally and physically. I didn't understand why my mind was betraying me over and over.

Finally, a few months later, I received a call saying that I'd been assigned to a counselor. I sat down on my counselor's comfy turquoise couch one Thursday morning. She asked a few questions, and I responded awkwardly. I told her about the lack of sleep I'd had lately and how I felt like I was going insane. Her face didn't show much expression and she wasn't rattled by what I said. She made me feel like it was perfectly reasonable that I would feel afraid if I knew of other break-ins happening around our house and didn't feel safe.

I didn't feel like myself with all of the lack of sleep. I was crying constantly and jumpy about every little thing. I showed up every other week to my counselor's office with the same story: I wasn't sleeping. What was she going to do about it?

She listened. She heard me out. She suggested that maybe I should consider moving houses. That was not something I had even considered. Where would we go? How would we break our lease? How would I find a house as nice yet affordable as this one? I heard her out week after week. I finally tipped over the edge after I watched a guy try to break into my car on my Ring camera three different times in one week.

My landlord was kind enough to let us out of our lease because she knew there was a lot of crime happening and that my roommates and I were scared. So we moved.

What would my counselor and I talk about now? That situation had consumed so much of the first few months of counseling. I felt certain I wouldn't need counseling much longer.

I don't know when the shift happened, but somewhere along the way, it felt like my counselor and I were almost friends. All she had to ask me was, "What's been going on?" and I would spill everything to her.

I feel like maybe I'm too easy of a client because I am not that hard of a girl to crack. If she's gonna listen, then I'm going to tell her.

I won't ever get used to spending 50 minutes talking about myself. Sometimes I feel a little guilty not asking her any questions back, but this isn't a coffee date with a new friend. It's a session with a counselor I'm paying for (Although I was very shocked the other day to learn that my counselor has had a boyfriend for six months and didn't think to tell me?!). I forget that I'm her client and not her friend. It's a weird balance.

Over the past year of counseling, we've talked through the ending of a job, the beginning of another job, the ending of a relationship, the fresh start of a relationship, mom having cancer, lack of sleep, and a whole lot more. I've learned about boundaries, asking the right questions, and doing what I feel is best and not what everyone is pushing me to do or wants for me. I know myself a little better now because of those 50-minute sessions with a woman I see a few times a month.

I'm a year in and I'm realizing that counseling can come and go in seasons. I'm currently at a place where I don't feel the need to go as often. I don't want to use it as a crutch, I want to use it as a tool in my toolbox in case I need an unbiased voice in my life.

Counseling isn't nearly as scary as I expected it to be. Having someone who is completely removed from every situation I find myself in is sometimes exactly what I need to see the stories I'm intertwined in from a bird's eye view. Maybe I'm not crazy or asking for too much or being unreasonable. My counselor never tells me what I should do, she just talks me through what my options are and how I feel about what's going on in my life.

What I didn't know when I did that intake session was that I would then go on to work at a counseling center almost a year to the day later. I was able to see why counseling matters and why it's needed before landing a job fundraising for the best place in the world, Daystar Counseling Ministries - a Godwink I didn't know to expect.

———

Our bodies are temples. They are strong and resilient and carry us even when we feel like we can go no further. We have minds that are brilliant and that are full of information, more information than we were ever meant to know or contain.

Be kind with yourself and to yourself. In a world where anxiety and depression are at an all-time high, you are not alone if you feel like the world is painful and you can't seem to find your way out of the darkness. Ask for help. Tell your people what's going on. Hang on to hope. You are needed here. You have purpose and are special in ways no one else could ever be.

Chapter 8

CAREERS

I wanted to be an actress for the first decade of my life. I remember when I was little I told my dad that I did not intend on going to college (I was 8 and didn't know what college was, but it seemed like my dad very much wanted me to go to this college place) and that I was going to move to Los Angeles to become an actress. He told me I most certainly could do that *after* I graduated from college.

I eventually realized that acting was not in my future, although I think I was a terrific Anne Boleyn in the 9th-grade school play. I enhanced her style with braces, a few missing teeth, and my dress ripping clean down the back in the middle of the play. The true professional that I was, I held my hands behind my back the rest of the play holding on for dear life to the fabric that was keeping me from flashing the entire audience. Maybe I should have stuck with acting after all.

I then decided I wanted to be a special education teacher. I had shadowed a special education class for a semester in 8th grade and loved the kids in that class with my entire heart. I still keep up with some of them to this day. Amid the darkness that is middle school, those kids made me smile every single day. They made everybody feel like somebody, and their love and kindness to me and one another will be something I hold on to for the rest of my life.

But then I decided I wasn't certain if I could be locked into one specific job forever. My mom had been a teacher and even she said she wasn't sure if I would enjoy teaching every day forever. So I moved on to wanting to be a lawyer. Didn't everyone want to be a lawyer or doctor at some point? That was, yet again, a short-lived dream.

When I applied to Auburn, I was a Pre-Occupational Therapy major. Before I even got to Auburn, I switched to an Exploratory major. I then changed my major freshman year to Human Development and Family Studies with a focus on Child Life.

The hunt for a major wasn't over yet, though. At the end of freshman year, I switched yet again and finally landed on Public Relations.

Apparently, they don't make students do this anymore, but when I was at Auburn, every time I changed my major I had to go pick up my file from my respective college advisor and carry it over to the building where my new advisor was. I carried that little orange folder at first with such embarrassment, but by the time we got to the fourth major, I was an old pro with no care in the world.

Commitment issues? Maybe when it comes to a career path. I continually felt like I had not found the right major. I didn't want to get stuck in one career path and never be able to get out. I wanted flexibility and freedom. When I was on my third major and thinking about switching yet again, I felt like I needed to hone in on one major and stick with it. So I did what any sane college kid would do and went to the library and printed out a list of all the majors Auburn offered. All 150 of them.

One by one, I went through each major and marked out the ones that I knew I had absolutely no interest in. I couldn't mark through Aerospace Engineering and Accounting with red ink fast enough. I finally dwindled the list until two words stared back at me. Public Relations. Sounded like fun to me.

And it was. I loved my classes. Maybe it was because my major centered around communicating with people, so naturally, I was in classes with tons of hilarious extroverts.

In a whirlwind, I was all of a sudden a senior in college with no plan for what I wanted to do after graduation. The only plan I had was that no matter what I was going to Nashville. I have always been that kid who loves school, so naturally, I thought, "Why don't I go get my Master's?"

In what, you might ask? Well, I thought since I knew nothing about business, maybe I should learn and get an MBA. So, I did. Three months after I walked across the stage at Auburn with my undergrad diploma, I was sitting at Belmont in finance and accounting classes where I didn't have a clue what I was doing.

I graduated from Belmont University with my MBA in August 2020. I walked around my parent's pool in my cap and gown, garnering applause from my family as I virtually finished my degree. It was a really strange time to be entering the adult world. I went on spring break and then never went back to Belmont. I never saw some of my classmates from my cohort ever again. But I was excited to see where I landed a job and to be staying in Nashville.

Three months after graduation, I sat at my wooden desk in my forest green leather chair applying for jobs when a familiar notification flashed across the top of my screen: yet another rejection email. Finding a job after graduating from college is not for the faint of heart, but add on a global pandemic and thousands of people with tons of experience laid off fighting for the same positions as me... It adds a little spice to the fun, that's for sure.

I was now going on month three of countless interviews, rejections, being ghosted by several companies… and no end in sight. I begged God to open just one door. That's all I needed. I prayed that over and over. Just one door, God. That's all I want. I don't need endless options.

Everything goes out the window when a global pandemic happens. In November 2020, one of my mentors called me to say there was an opening at the nonprofit she works for, and she wanted me to consider applying for the position.

I was overjoyed because I KNEW God had finally answered my prayer. This had to be the job for me; I felt it in my bones.

I had my first-round interview with my mentor's organization and felt so good about it. They quickly moved on to a second-round interview with me. I didn't feel so good about that one. The questions felt cold and disconnected, and I didn't feel like I was able to talk about all of the ideas I had for the position and why I loved their mission. I hung up and cried, feeling so misled by God. Maybe He hadn't heard me after all.

Weeks went by, and I didn't hear a word. I reached out to see if there was any update and was told that 112 people had applied for the position and they were still interviewing several candidates. 112 people?!? I knew I was done for. I had no experience and was aware that many people with years of work history had been laid off during the pandemic and were fighting for the same job as me.

A month passed by after my second interview and still no word. Christmas was right around the corner. Christmas is usually my favorite time of the year, but all of the shops and homes covered in lush wreaths and twinkly bright lights couldn't lift my spirits. Three days before Christmas, I sat with my mom in the drive-thru of Firehouse Subs (I'm sorry, but for some reason knowing Firehouse Subs is a part of this serious moment makes me laugh) and I saw my phone light up with my mentor's name across it.

I immediately ignored it. Another job I had applied for and interviewed for had rejected me that morning, and I was not in the mood for another rejection. It had been over a month since my last interview with my mentor's organization and since it had been so long I was certain they had chosen someone else for the role.

As my mom and I waited on our subs, I listened to the voicemail my mentor left me and the only words I heard were, "I have an early Christmas gift to offer you!"

I was certain it was probably some kind of part-time job or an idea of somewhere else to apply because she had offered the job to someone else and felt bad and wanted to help me.

I tried to call her back, but she texted me to say she would have to call me back after work. It felt like the longest day waiting for her to call me, but she finally did. She told me the full-time job at her nonprofit was mine and she wanted me to take it and work with her. I couldn't believe it; I was stunned into tears and silence. I was overjoyed that the hunt was over, and maybe God had heard my prayer after all.

When you think about your dream job, what does it look like? For me, I wanted to have a direct impact on those who need care and services they couldn't otherwise afford. I wanted to write wherever and however I could, sharing my experiences with God with others. I didn't know what that would look like and what I'm looking for shifts as I learn and grow.

All I do know is God shows up in places and spaces that seem unexpected. God reveals what we need when we need it. It drives me insane because I crave instant gratification, but now a handful of years removed from my first job hunt I'm so grateful for what I learned about myself when I couldn't find a job. I learned I am resilient, that God's best sometimes takes longer than what I think is best for me and that He has not forgotten me.

———

I felt a shift in my heart about my most recent job on a Tuesday afternoon. My entire department had quit in two months. It was hard and horrible and heartbreaking because I adored my team. My boss was my hero. It was our busiest time of year for fundraising, and I was drowning. But that wasn't my breaking point.

With no team left, I was trying to fill as many gaps as I could, gaps that our organization could and couldn't see. I now can pinpoint so many moments that could have been the time when I walked away, but the day that did it for me was an ordinary afternoon at work. I was helping a co-worker with a project that normally wouldn't have been hers, but with so many resignations of other co-workers lately, she was left to do this task. She asked for my assistance, and I was glad to give it. I loved this co-worker dearly and we were both trying to keep everything together in our respective departments.

We were powering through the project, knocking it out, and we called the person who we were to turn the project into to see what her thoughts were so far and ask some follow-up questions. This woman picked up the phone and from start to finish she was belittling and made me feel mortifyingly stupid, piercing us with her words that aren't worth repeating or reliving.

It wasn't the first time this had happened with this person. I was stunned at the tone in which she spoke to me and the words she said, but I wasn't surprised. And in that moment, I felt released from working at this place. The work we were doing was phenomenal, but it was extremely hard and the burnout was so, so real. Add on situation after situation of unappreciation and disrespect, and I felt myself crumbling into a shell of who I was.

I started looking for jobs, but weeks went by and I didn't find anything that I felt passionate about. I felt so frustrated. Why did I feel like God was calling me out of a place, yet I couldn't find anything that felt right?

As time continued to pass, situations continued to unfold at my job that left me feeling devastated each time I left work. I felt beaten down. I had tension headaches frequently, and my left eye was twitching every single day.

I sat with a mentor and friend of mine over chips and creamy jalapeño sauce at Chuy's and told her of my frustrations. As I told her about everything that was going on, she said, "Do you think you'd be interested in working at Daystar?"

I didn't know much about this faith-based counseling center for kids but what I had heard about them were the best and brightest stories. Daystar seemed like a place full of hope from what little I knew. And selfishly, I could use some hope after the past six months of my job. But I looked at their website and didn't see any job postings. My mentor encouraged me to reach out anyway.

I sent a cold email later that weekend to a staff member at Daystar with my resume attached, telling them a little bit about me and my interest in a development role if they ever had any openings.

I didn't expect a reply to a cold email. I was also having flashbacks to my job hunt during the pandemic. But not even twenty-four hours later I found myself sitting in a little yellow house with the woman I had emailed from Daystar. We chatted and she told me they had been thinking about hiring in development and showed me a job description. I read it and felt my hopes sink a little. I felt like I might be overqualified for the job.

I left and didn't know if I'd return for another interview since it didn't seem like they were hiring for someone within my skill set. They asked me to come back in for a second interview and further discuss a position with them. I semi-reluctantly returned, wishing they had a role that aligned more with what I was looking for. I met with another development staff member and then with Daystar's founder.

As I talked with the founder, Melissa, I felt right at home. She was a clever, kind woman with a dog named Happy Meal trailing not too far behind her. When she came into the room, she immediately hugged me. I knew from that moment that we'd be friends. I am quite frankly over stern handshakes and formal introductions anyway.

We talked for close to an hour about everything: my family, what I could bring to the table, why I was leaving my current job, and what the position could be like that they might create for me. I was sold as we talked, but I knew this was it for me as I got up to leave and she asked if she could pray for me. As she prayed, she asked that God would lead me to the right position whether that was with them or somewhere else, and that she already loved me.

One of my favorite quotes from author and speaker Priscilla Shirer is, "Waiting is not the same thing as inactivity. Waiting is a commitment to continue in obedience until God speaks."[11] I left Daystar bouncing off the walls with excitement, feeling like I finally had been led to the right place. I actively waited for Him to move me. I sent the email and hoped God would do the rest.

What matters to you when it comes to your job? Here are some qualities that matter to me:

▸ Meaningful and challenging work

▸ Fair and competitive salary

▸ Work/life balance is encouraged

▸ Healthy and vibrant company culture

▸ Professional development is promoted

▸ Strong benefits package (insurance ain't cheap!)

▸ A medium-sized company is usually my preference

What's on your list? Pray over those qualities. Keep a sticky note or note card on your mirror and actively pray over those qualities in a position and organization. God cares about the details even if they seem small. A wild wish I hoped for in my next job was being able to have a day during the week to write, but that seemed like a far-off possibility if I wanted to still make a full-time salary.

When I got the offer from Daystar, my schedule was for 4 days a week with every Friday off... what? Never working a Friday again? I'm never leaving this place. I was a full-time employee and making more than my last job! I couldn't believe it. A wish whispered under my breath came to life and, in turn, created room for me to write this book. Life is wild, y'all.

Are you ready for a change? Talk to your friends and mentors about it. Do they know of any organizations that might be a good fit for you based on the qualities you listed? You'd be surprised by what people's answers are and what connections they have. Make a list of places you'd be interested in working one day. Keep a note of it on your phone to refer back to in the future. I've kept a running list for years because you never know when you may need to begin your job hunt, and I never want to forget about places that I have heard of that sound like a potential good fit.

———

I remember as a child I did well in school, so some people automatically thought I should be a doctor. I had no interest in medicine. Zero, zilch, none. I would've never enjoyed it or done well in it because I lacked passion and purpose for that kind of career. God hadn't wired me for medicine. We can't let people heavily influence how we spend the majority of our days. You know what's best for you. I've watched friends pick careers because it's what their parents wanted for them, but they're miserable. We need guidance from our people, sure, but I have a feeling you know in your gut what kind of career you *don't* want, even if you don't know yet what you *do* want.

Committing our work, which takes up most of our days, to the Lord establishes our thoughts and plans on solid ground. The foundation is firm regardless of how we're treated at work. He's unshakeable, so when our environment becomes chaotic, He is our peace. And with the Holy Spirit as our guide, we will know when it's time to go.

Who we are is not based on what we do for a living; it's so much more than that. God's looking for how we glorify Him in not only our jobs but also our friendships, relationships, how we spend our free time, the way we speak about others, and a million other ways.

Our occupations shouldn't be something that drains the life out of us, yet I see so many friends left running on empty because of the work they do. I didn't realize how bad it had gotten at my old job until I was able to remove myself from that place. I had gotten almost used to always feeling anxious at work, and now I feel a million times lighter and freer.

A verse I come back to time and time again is Colossians 3:23, *"Whatever you do, work heartily, as for the Lord and not for men."* In whatever we do and in *all* that we do, God wants to be glorified. Our career isn't the sole way to honor God. He wants us to glorify Him in our work, but I don't believe He is looking for us to overwork ourselves.

Jesus teaches us 37 parables throughout the Gospels. 32 out of the 37 parables are about work.[12] Isn't that kind of crazy? Jesus cares about the work you and I do, so much so that He spoke about it in 32 parables during his ministry.

Before Jesus started His ministry, He was a carpenter. He had a profession that maybe didn't seem the most glamorous, but it was exactly where He was supposed to be. Keep an open mind to the possibilities of where God might lead you. Talk to your people about what you're looking for, and be a connector for those looking for a job. We all need each other to bridge the gap between societal and personal pressures and the direction where God is leading us.

Maybe you're in a job you don't love but don't necessarily feel called out of yet. Look around and ask yourself, "How is Christ already here in this job?" How can you see Him moving and present in your organization? How can you join Jesus in spreading His light to those you interact with at work? I bet you'd be surprised what might happen when you try to stop auto-piloting through your work days and look for opportunities to be a part of what Jesus is already doing at your workplace. He's already there regardless of whether it's the best or worst job you've ever had, so join Him in furthering His kingdom in every crevice. Jesus hasn't called us to an easy life but to a life worth living, a good life. I'm expectant and hopeful for the places He is preparing us for.

Chapter 9

THE THIEF OF JOY

Tucked under the bottom right corner of my desk at work are three Polaroid pictures: one of me with my dad cheesing real big, a solo shot of me decked out in hot pink and green clothing with a feather boa and crown, and the last is a picture of me with some of my best friends before the Iron Bowl, Auburn's annual football game against Alabama, in 2017. Three little moments. Each picture holds a memory that is ingrained in my mind forever. Happy, raw moments.

Something's so special about Polaroids. You don't get a do-over. You only have one shot to get the picture before it slowly bubbles into a photo right before your eyes. I have never looked at a Polaroid picture that I'm in and thought, "I hate that picture of myself" because the moment itself is so unfiltered.

I scroll through my social media to perfectly curated pictures of perfectly curated moments. Not a hair out of place, not a smudge on the photo lens. The best and brightest moments of my closest 2000 friends. It's a weird thing, isn't it? Being so closely connected to people you barely know.

Not a lot of raw and unfiltered moments fill my feed, and I won't pretend like I've been filling mine with those kinds of moments either. But I want to. I want to stop being envious of other people's lives when what is in front of me in my everyday life is so good, special, and unique to me. I love my life. I genuinely do for the first time in a long time. But every minute I spend scrolling through social media leaves me feeling empty and discontent, wanting to have my life match the person I'm staring at on my screen.

So how do we break the cycle of comparison? Spoiler alert: I can't think of anything more in the world I'd rather do than delete my social media, but with work and writing and a million reasons in between I don't feel like it is possible to do so. I am sure I'm not the only one. So many of my friends need it for their jobs or to keep up with friends they never see. If it isn't realistic to get rid of these crazy apps, what do we do?

After I meet someone, I am quick to size them up. Too pretty and intimidating? Doubt they are nice, we probably won't be friends. In reality, I am probably often protecting myself from those who I think would reject me as their friend. So many times I've been proven wrong. People don't judge you the way that you think they do. I'm often my own worst enemy.

I feel this real sense of urgency to be the "on girl." I struggle with slowing down and my mind can never keep up. We lose ourselves in busyness trying to compete with those around us. Maybe the anxiety we all feel and the stress that crushes our souls stems from the fact that rest isn't a priority in our lives but busyness is.

A couple of weeks ago I was in my room on a Saturday where I had nothing to do for the first time in months. No agenda, no plans, just what I wanted to do all alone. I was lying in my bed watching Netflix when I had this wave of anxiety overtake me. I had no idea why I felt so anxious. I felt my mind spiraling completely out of control.

My body had no idea what to do going from pushing 80+ mph in a 35 mph speed limit and then slamming on brakes to 0. Our bodies weren't meant to be constantly exhausted and pushed past our limits emotionally, physically, and mentally. Sometimes I feel like I'm skating over barely frozen ice hoping it can hold my body weight. On that Saturday, I slipped straight through the ice and couldn't find my way back out of the water.

I've been processing a lot lately about what is important to me and wondering if those things are important to God. I feel certain that what is important to me matters to God, but I also believe He knows that some of the things I care about are worldly and have a deeper impact on me than I realized.

Success seems to be defined by how much money you have, what kind of house you buy, or what your relationships and friendships look like on social media. But I'm beginning to wonder if I'm brave enough to start doing the work of changing what matters to me to be what matters the most to God. Am I caring for my soul? Am I scratching more than the surface in my friendships and relationships or am I emotionally unavailable to go deep?

It's a scary thing to be known, to be fully known, and in a big city, it's too easy to be a little fish in a big pond and stay undetected, under the radar.

I know that the Lord is doing some refining in me and some much-needed stripping of what no longer needs to remain in my life. He is pulling back layers that I thought I had buried deep and had no need to revisit.

I haven't spent much time talking to God lately, and I'm starting to wonder if that's because I know He has something better in store for me and I don't feel like I want whatever that may be.

My life looks very different than I thought it would at this age. I have tried to write my own story beginning at the end of the book without inviting God in. I have been holding my fist clenched and I'm slowly trying to open my fists.

I pray that I won't live a half-lived life because of my selfish desires. I pray that I'll be known fully and deeply, know others fully and deeply, and not shy away from the hard questions.

At the beginning of the year, the Spiritual Wellness Coordinator at my job gave us the opportunity to be assigned "star words," which is a word that will define what the year will bring and what we will bring to the year. Star words are a growing Epiphany tradition, one I had never heard of until my co-worker taught me about them.

I love all of this kind of stuff. Assign me a personality test or some kind of quiz to give me the words that I need to hear or the answers I am looking for and I am all for it. So

I said yes to being assigned a star word and gave no other comments or feedback about it.

One day, I found a manila envelope with my word for the year lying on my desk. I was expecting it to be, you know, one of the fruits of the spirit. Love, joy, peace, patience... you know the drill. I don't know why that was what I thought star words would be, but instead what I opened was the word "search" scribbled on a gold paper star. It caught me a little bit off guard. Where did I need to search? And what exactly was I supposed to search for?

I've now recognized that I've had a lot of searching to do. I've had to search for a new job, a new place to live, and a church home. I've had to seek balance in my life and hope in dark places and peace within circumstances I could not understand. I'm searching and hoping and dreaming that I'll grow less encumbered with what everyone else is doing and more in love with my life. This search isn't the search I thought it would be going on, but I sure am better for it.

Do you remember when Instagram sold verification checks and you could become "verified," giving you a tiny blue check by your name? I watched as people I knew gained those little checks by their names and I was so confused. Has everyone I have ever known become famous overnight?

Instagram sold 44 million blue checks in one day for $15 per month.[13] In those first 24 hours of selling verifications, Instagram made $660 million.

Everybody wants to be somebody. We want to feel important like we're at the top of the food chain. We want to feel known and seen, even on social media. We're trying to fill a void that can only really be satisfied by Jesus.

I feel my world in orbit, and I want it to be spinning around Jesus, but sometimes I feel myself placing value in other areas. I want people to think I am funny or smart or that I'm going places and making a name for myself.

When each of us was born, one of the first questions asked about you and me was probably what our name would be. More than likely, your parents had thought long and hard about what they would call you.

It's one of the most sacred words we carry with us for the rest of our lives. Our names tell people who we are and each name has a meaning.

In the first book of the Bible, the name used for God is "Elohim," but after chapter 2, His name shifts to "YHWH Elohim," which means Lord God in English. In a study I'm working through, I learned that Lord God is the covenant name of God, showing that He is personal and has a relationship with the people He created.

God then gives Adam the ability to name all of the animals, and while Adam names the animals, he isn't naming them by what they will be called, but rather on what these animals will become.

After reading this, I looked up what my name means, and I might be in trouble if I start living up to my name. While the root meaning of my name has a good meaning (beloved), the actual word meaning for Mary is rebellious/bitter.

I hope I'm becoming more beloved than bitter, but my heart certainly doesn't always reflect that.

You would think having a double name wouldn't be that difficult for people to understand, but it is. My whole life people have asked if they could call me something shorter, something simpler. (Which is kind of offensive because… this is my name?) This stumbling block for people unwilling to say four syllables has resulted in a lot of nicknames.

The summer I lived in Nashville my new boss really couldn't get behind any of the nicknames people had picked out for me over the years. MSV? Nope. Mencer? No shot. And then as if she had an awakening deep in her soul, she blurted out "SPENCE." To which I questioned, "Spence?" And she said, "YES, SPENCE. Like SUSPENSE." And so Spence was born.

After yet another nickname, I started thinking more about the names I call myself. Some days, the words that run through my head are clever, loving, or fun, while other times, I'm quick to call myself things like lazy, unworthy, and ugly.

Am I becoming what I call myself? If I call myself by names that the Lord wouldn't call me, I'm working on becoming more of what the world wants me to believe about myself rather than what the King of the world wants me to believe about me, His creation.

Names hold power. In fact, in one of my favorite books, *How to Win Friends and Influence People*, Dale Carnegie says, "A person's name is to that person the sweetest and most important sound in any language."[14] When someone calls your name, you immediately turn or perk up or move toward the person who is speaking to you. In our everyday moments, the Lord is calling our names, speaking to us. Urging us toward Himself, reminding us that we were made in His image. We are reflectors of God.

Often, names are repeated twice by Jesus when He is speaking to someone. Jesus does this as a sign of affection toward the people He loves, but He also tends to do this while gently correcting them in some way. Jesus does this to show compassion followed by conviction.

I want to work toward calling myself by the names God has defined me by: worthy, loved, chosen, in His image, His daughter. I'll leave behind the old names like the sweaters we shed when winter ends.

And maybe we can work on changing what we call other people. Are we defining others by the characteristics God has designed them with or are we quick to point out the wrong in someone else when we really should be turning to ourselves and working on our own change? My heart needs some work, this I know.

For me, it comes down to four elements when I am experiencing such painful comparison to others:

1. LACKING COMPASSION FOR MYSELF.

I am constantly working on being kinder to myself. When someone compliments me, I need to believe them. When I experience someone else winning, I need to cheer for them. I need to love and be loved by myself and by others. I need to allow the trickling down of truth coming from heaven to fill up my cup.

2. LEAVING COMMUNITY OUT OF THE EQUATION.

When I begin to compare myself to others, I need to talk to a trusted friend about it. Words of comparison spoken out loud lose their power, especially when they are entrusted with a dear friend.

3. LOSING THE COURAGE OF MY CONVICTIONS.

God created you and me on, for, and with purpose. I believe what God has written and said about me, but am I living a life that reflects those beliefs? Some days are easier than others when it comes to this. I need to root myself in truth, in Scripture, and be reminded of what all God has to say about you and me and why it matters to be wildly in love with who I was created to be.

4. LEANING INTO A FALSE SENSE OF CONNECTION.

Social media doesn't paint the full picture; it paints the picture we want everyone to see. Someone's highlight may be hiding the pain happening behind the scenes. Spending less and less time on the Internet gives me less to compare myself to. Social media pushes us to feel connected to galleries of smiling faces and wishing we were someone or somewhere else, but we all have our own battles behind screens. Reminding myself of that removes the false sense of reality social media has given me.

Today, I was scrolling through social media and somehow found myself looking through this stranger's Instagram account. I'm not even sure how I found her page. She was getting ready to launch her first book and was posting tons and tons of content about it. One of her goals is to make the *New York Times* bestseller list. I immediately envied her and hoped she wouldn't make it.

And then I caught myself. Why would I wish that on anyone... but especially a stranger who's probably poured so much into writing this book? Why was that my first thought anyway?

Because she has the courage and confidence to speak the dreams I wouldn't dare utter out loud. She's not afraid of telling the world about her dream even with the potential of failing. I want that kind of courage. What I see in this girl I don't know is confidence in Christ that gives her the courage to speak out loud her deepest desires because even if they don't come true, God has her best interests at heart and will not fail her.

So, I followed this stranger and cheered her on while she launched her book into the world because her words, dreams, and calling matter. And I know there is enough room in the world for both of us.

At my former job with a women's addiction treatment center, I led a creative writing group every other week with some of the clients. Many of them would come in saying that they are not writers and will not be able to do this class. Over and over I would tell them about how they would surprise themselves. Everyone is a writer.

One afternoon, a client came in talking about how she could not write. I promised her the assignment wouldn't be difficult, and that the fun thing about writing is there isn't a right or wrong to do it. Your story gets to be what you want it to be!

I decided to start with a lighthearted writing prompt: *Would you rather be able to fly or be invisible? Then, write a story about you using your superpower for good.*

I expected the stories to be fun, and most of them were. But one client's story, the very same client who told me she could not write, took my breath away.

She began her story by flying to different places to help people she knew but quickly it turned serious and she said, "If I could fly I would fly to a place called Grace and God would meet me there."

The story continued, and she met God along the way, but I don't know if I heard much else after her line about flying to a place called Grace. What I would give to easily fly and land there. Where is this place called Grace? Do we need wings to get there? Can God shower me in grace right now, right here?

I haven't been able to stop thinking about it. I could picture it, her flying with pearly white wings to this beautiful, simple destination where God met her and clothed her in love and splendor.

Why do I keep waiting to fly there? Grace isn't a gated community or tucked away in an unreached place, it's right here. I hold out my hand and hope God will intertwine His hand with mine and take me there.

I've felt more humbled and knocked down lately than I've felt in a long time. In a lot of ways, it's been really freeing. I've had to rely on God like I haven't had to in years.

Disappointment has been like broken glass all around me, my feet and hands are bruised and cut, but I wouldn't change a moment of the past few months. The pain has been ugly, but it left me no choice but to join God in this place called Grace. I can't survive without His Grace, and I can't fully experience a life worth living without the good, bad, and ugly. This hard time will be a holy time, that I'm sure of.

In this place called Grace, God is there waiting for you and me. He's not dwelling in the past; He's fully alive in the present. He's not comparing our stories, our lives, our situations to anyone else. We were created on purpose for a purpose.

I'm opening my hands today, asking God to let me join Him in this place called Grace because I can't imagine where I can be more alive or free from comparison. I am who He says I am. I want to believe it.

Chapter 10

HOBBIES

"**D**oes anyone want to take adult ice skating lessons with me?"

I clicked send on that sentence to a group message with some of my girlfriends in Nashville. My whole life, I had been dreaming of taking ice skating lessons. I have *Ice Princess* to thank for my obsession with ice skating. I know you'll be surprised by this, but we did not have any ice skating rinks in South Georgia while I was growing up, so after viewing that movie, I made my own ice skating rink. I downloaded the movie soundtrack to my lime green iPod nano, jammed my feet into my pink and black roller skates, and made my way up and down our short driveway. I twisted and twirled, pretending I was an ice skater in the summer heat.

As I got older, I vowed that if I ever lived in a city with an ice skating rink, I was going to take lessons. I am a girl of my word, so at the ripe age of 26, I signed up for seven weeks of ice skating lessons with one of my best friends, Savannah. She was planning her wedding and getting ready to move to Atlanta, so what we didn't say is that ice skating was also our excuse to see each other once a week before she left me for a new start in a new city.

We showed up to the rink bundled up in our warmest sweaters and knitted beanies, ready for the class ahead. We laced up our well-worn rental skates and went to meet our instructor, a small, older man with salt and pepper hair who we would learn didn't believe in smiling and certainly was not amused by us.

Our class had all sorts of different characters: a handful of high school girls, a mother and her adult daughter, a 6-foot burly man who had aspirations of learning to play hockey after figuring out the basics of ice skating... and then there was me and Savannah.

For seven weeks, we showed up for our lessons, learning all of the ice skating fundamentals. I counted down the days until our ice skating lessons every single week. It wasn't work-related, and I wasn't sitting around on my phone in the afternoons. I was learning a new skill, one I had always hoped to learn. By the end, I could skate backward, skate in a circle on one foot, and move all around the rink. Kristi Yamaguchi better watch out. I was sad when the lessons ended, but I had another item on my wish list of new skills I wanted to learn.

Next up: hip hop classes. I love to dance, although I'm not very sure I'm good at it. I signed my roommate Brooke and I up for a hip-hop class one night after work, and we drove over to this studio that we knew nothing about. It looked legit on Instagram, so it had to be safe, right?

Going with Brooke was a bit of a mistake. A trained dancer growing up, she knew all of the choreography before I had grasped the four first moves, but I didn't care. I was having so much fun that nothing else mattered.

At the end of the class, we had to break into groups and perform the dance. This was my nightmare scenario, but as the adult that I am, I wasn't about to run out of the room in fear. Although I did contemplate it.

I jumped in with my group and did probably about half of the dance. I was content with just doing my best and not being the best. As an overly competitive person, this was a new concept for me. It was fun doing something with no expectations for myself except to just have a good time.

This is what hobbies are for. It's not something I have to shine at; it's an activity that makes my heart smile and feel alive. It brings a little piece of my inner kid to the surface. I didn't realize how important hobbies were until I started spending the majority of my days on a computer at work.

We have to fight for time with our hobbies. You have to try lots of different things until they stick. Hobbies come and go and some may be around for life.

A new one I, along with the rest of the country, am trying out is pickleball. Can I be honest, though? I do not want to be one of those crazy pickleball people who stand in the kitchen all day just slamming it back and forth. I want to be a leisurely, very average beginner bopping it across the court not having to think too quickly about my next step. Hit me up if you want to play on my level.

What's something you always dreamed of doing as a child? Gymnastics lessons? They have those for adults.

Horseback riding? Call my sister, she's a horse girl and would be happy to teach you the ropes. Sewing? I promise you someone is teaching that skill in your community. Google can help you find them. Studies show that having a hobby can reduce stress, enhance well-being, improve social connection and mental health, and decrease depression and anxiety.[15]

Hobbies don't have to be something you do every day. Look at your calendar and schedule a few hours for fun each week: painting for an hour on Saturday morning or LARPing once every few weeks after work on Tuesdays.

Some of you may be wondering what the heck LARPing is, and it would be my honor to tell you about it because I was unfamiliar with this hobby until one Thursday morning in my undergrad Fiction Writing class.

We wandered into our class and took our seats, but our professor was nowhere to be found. Instead, this man who was a stranger to us, sat on our professor's desk and told us he would be our substitute teacher for the day.

I'd never had a sub in college, and I didn't know anyone who had but I just rolled with it. Our substitute professor asked us to go around and introduce ourselves, like it was the first day of class, and tell him one activity we like to do for fun.

We slowly made our way around the class, and the guy next to me said, "Hi, I'm Jacob and I really enjoy LARPing!"

Half of my classes nodded along, but I didn't understand. So naively, I asked, "What is LARPing?"

You would've thought I had asked what planet we lived on or who the president was. Every head in the class turned to look at me, stunned that I was unfamiliar with LARPing.

Jacob quickly looked at me and said, "Live Action Role Playing. You've never LARPed before?"

Couldn't say I had, Jacob.

Finally, the attention turned away from me because the girl next to Jacob said, "My name is Scottie and I'm actually a seamstress for LARPers!"

I think Jacob and Scottie fell in love right then and there. No joke, they both pulled out business cards for their LARPing escapades. I looked around for cameras. This couldn't be real.

Jacob invited me to join him at the park on Tuesdays after class for some LARPing fun, but I never took him up on it. I regret it to this day.

Hobbies come in all different forms, LARPing, collecting stamps, or writing poetry. Sometimes, we've got to think outside the box to find a hobby that's fun to us. If you're anything like me, I get into autopilot mode in my downtime trying to do something mindless like scroll through social media or watch reruns of *The Bachelor*. Channeling our energy into something that slows our minds and bodies down feeds us in a way social media and TV can't. We want to rewire our brains to crave nourishing hobbies instead of mindless activities that leave us more depressed, disconnected, and disassociated.

Finding a hobby we enjoy lets the chemical messengers in our brain (known as neurotransmitters) release dopamine, which makes us want to do this activity over and over again. Research also shows that some musical hobbies can improve your memory and some artistic hobbies like reading or board game puzzles can prevent dementia as we grow older.[16]

Additionally, hobbies can help us relive positive memories from our childhood reminding us of simpler times. Happiness anchors from our childhood can nudge us to not take life so seriously and to enjoy the little moments.

With many of us in jobs and careers that have big, daunting projects that sometimes take months or even years to complete, having a hobby that provides us with a finished product every time can show us that we are more than capable of starting what we finish. As someone who loves nothing more than a project seen to completion, hobbies show me that I am capable of learning new skills, completing small tasks, and having fun while doing it.

Little joy wins matter to me and make a difference in a life that can feel too serious. We weren't meant to only find joy in extracurricular activities as children and even as college kids. Joy awaits in those same moments as an adult too. I refuse to believe that God created us to only have the happiest moments of our lives during the first quarter of our existence. We might have to work a little harder to find fun in the real world, but it matters to seek fun out.

––––––

I've been skiing twice in my life. The first time I went skiing, I was in Jackson Hole, Wyoming. I stepped off the plane at 18 years old, overjoyed for my first true interaction with snow. It had snowed a few times in my childhood, but it typically always melted before too much fun could be had. It would be different here in this snow-filled city.

I had always wanted to go snow skiing. It seemed magical gliding down the slopes of white powdery snow. I had grown up water skiing in South Georgia, and my dad told me that I absolutely would not need ski lessons as I was an excellent water skier.

I am here to tell you that being an excellent water skier has nothing to do with one's ability to ski on mountains of snow.

Jackson Hole is not exactly a beginner's kind of place to go. Here is the singular problem with having parents who have instilled fearlessness in your soul: I believe everything will be fun and easy. Skiing is not that.

I got off the ski lift and immediately had no idea how to stop. I skied off into the abyss of snow at the edge of the mountain and wiped out. I laid there for quite some time because I was a couple of feet deep in snow. A snowmobile finally appeared and a very kind man lifted me up by my arms out of the sparkling white snow. He asked if I was okay and I said, "Yes, thank you!" and carried on my way, too embarrassed to say much more.

Panic rose in my chest realizing I still had miles of skiing left before I'd reach the bottom. My family was nowhere to be found because, if you recall, they were not worried about me picking up snow skiing at the ripe old age of 18. I was going to have to figure this out myself.

And at this time I'd like to say I took some deep breaths, collected myself, and went along my merry way. But that is not at all what I did. Afraid and alone on the mountain, tears streaked my cheeks, freezing on my rosy face. I was so mad at my dad for giving me no instructions and not preparing me for what lay ahead.

Hundreds of people skied past me, not even seeing me. They kept their eyes focused on what was ahead. I watched as they all seemed to glide with ease. Even the little six-year-olds in their rainbow ski suits were putting me to shame. I wanted to climb back up the mountain and hop on the next ski lift, but there is no turning back when you're going down a mountain covered in powder.

I went skiing once more four years later with some of my college best friends in one of the most beautiful places I've ever been: Banff, Canada. We got ski passes off Groupon and made our way up the slopes. I was older and wiser and ready to do this. I had gotten better toward the end of my first skiing trip so I thought I would be even better this time, but I wasn't. I should have known it was not going to end well when I realized I had my helmet on backward as we were going down the slopes.

When I felt like I was really out of control, I would just fall to the side into the snow instead of trying to stop pizza-style with my skis. I would rather know I'm going to stop and do it myself than wipe out uncontrollably. I didn't want to hope my feet somehow magically made this pizza everyone talks about to stop. I did not trust myself that I could make it down the mountain. I would set myself up to fail.

And I do that in my mind too. I set myself up to fail, that everyone is against me, and that I'm not enough. I want to know the ending long before I get there.

As I neared the end of the mountain on my last run that trip, I fell down and laughed. I recognized the fear instilled in me of failing and spinning out of control carries over into my everyday life. I grasp control of situations and all the prying in the world won't rip away the grip I have on life.

Well, until the Lord intervenes and knocks the breath out of me to wake me up and show me that He's got this. I can just glide on into what He's laid before me, into the unknown, knowing that He knows better, or I can lay in the snow and watch others pass me by with smiles on their faces.

I tried and did not succeed when it came to skiing. I can confidently say that will not be my hobby of choice moving forward; however, I have had to make peace with the fact that I need to get comfortable trying new things and not immediately becoming the next Olympic skier. A culture of instant gratification and a mindset that seeks perfectionism can be a recipe for disaster when trying a new hobby, but something about pushing through the awkwardness of a new activity brings a sense of accomplishment that sharpens us.

———

If you're wondering, "Mary Spencer, that sounds great and all but I don't even know where to begin with finding a hobby," I hear you and I have some ideas.

1. **Revisit those childhood dreams.** Have you always wanted to play the guitar? What about playing lacrosse? Wish you had been a ballet dancer? Jot down some of the activities you wish you had done

in your childhood and see what your city has to offer when it comes to doing these activities as an adult.

2. **Explore the resources in your community.** You'd be surprised what you'd see being advertised on your YMCA's bulletin board on Facebook or even in a mass email about what's going on in your city weekly.

3. **Invite a friend in on a new hobby.** Talk to a friend that you would love seeing on a more consistent basis and see what y'all could commit to weekly or monthly doing together. They may have an idea that you haven't thought of yet!

4. **Prioritize enjoyment over perfection.** Do you think it'd be fun to take a creative writing class but have never written anything besides school papers? Who cares? No one is going to think twice about how much experience you have when it comes to something that's a hobby of yours.

Life feels so serious as an adult, and we need an escape from all the craziness in our lives and in our hearts. I've gotten to know the Lord better through some of my hobbies because I know that the Lord embodies joy, and I see a sliver of joy when I immerse myself in a hobby. Hobbies help us get closer to becoming the people we were meant to be: full of wondrous, childlike delight.

Chapter 11

TRYING TO TRUST GOD

I looked over at my dog, Cosby, a black labradoodle who always wears a mischievous grin on his face, weighing sixty-five pounds of fur and love, and I knew what was coming next. It always starts with him getting up from where he's lying and starting to high-step like a Tennessee Walking horse. Then, he falls over, and his whole body begins to seize. You can't stop seizures; you just have to wait for it to pass and hold him tight.

Cosby has had epilepsy for several years. I won't lie to you, there have been times when a seizure happened, and I got up and left until his little body stopped seizing. Sometimes it feels too hard to watch, knowing there is nothing I can do to stop what's happening. I leave and let my sister or parents take care of him. As the years have passed, I've grown more accustomed to his epilepsy. I don't get up and leave, although I want to. I just sit there with him, comforting him the best I know how.

I find myself asking God on my hard days if He has gotten up and walked away during my seizing, in the hard moments of my life where I feel like I'm being held captive to fear, unable to move forward. Is it too hard for Him to watch us when we choose the world over Him more often than not?

I used to think the harder I fought falling out on the ground, the more power I had. Now I'm seeing that on days where I feel like I can't pick myself up off the floor, God is there lying with me. He's holding me close, pulling me in, and not letting me go, even after the seizing has finished. He is asking for my heart and hands to be surrendered. That's when the real work can begin.

———

The first vivid memory of grief I have is when my Papa passed away after battling lung cancer for two years. My 13-year-old heart was broken, but I remember his funeral and the days after his passing with bittersweet memories: running around with my cousins in his backyard, eating yummy casseroles people had cooked and dropped off for us, and playing the piano at his funeral. It was a hard, sad week, but I feel like we celebrated his life well. I grieved losing him, but I also found joy in knowing that I would see him again in heaven one day.

The year I lost my Papa was a year full of grieving. Losing him and losing friends. 7th grade was a brutal, ugly year, and I remember feeling a new kind of heartbreak when none of my friends came to my Papa's visitation. One by one, my sister and all of my cousins had friends come to see them, but none of my friends came to be there for me. It hurt me twice over: I had lost my Papa and maybe I didn't have any best friends after all.

I decided after that it may be time to find some new friends, so I started hanging out with some different girls at school. A girl I had thought previously to be one of my closest friends, Sabrina, did not like that I was no longer hanging out with her and she was set on making that known.

One night shortly after Papa's funeral I was at my little sister's school musical.

I sat with some girls I had recently started hanging out with more, and Sabrina wasn't thrilled about me sitting with someone besides her. In the middle of the show, Sabrina stormed over to me and screamed at me words I will never forget: **"No one cares about your dead grandpa."**

It's hard for me to keep writing. What do you say after that? Even after 13 years? Those words gutted me. They still bring tears to my eyes each time I think about them.

I'll never be able to forget those words or the apology I never received. I have to actively work on forgiveness every single time that I think about those seven words strung along into a sentence I could never unhear.

Attending a small private school has its pros and cons, one con being you can't escape the people you're in school with. You have a fight with a friend? Better figure it out or things are going to be awkward at school because there are only 55 people in your grade. You and your boyfriend break up? Hope y'all can stay friends because you may end up being lab partners. Sabrina and I were going to have to figure out a way to get through this. We were going to be around each other and in each other's lives for years to come.

Once we got to high school, we were in most of the same classes, in a lot of the same extracurriculars, and were partners for a ton of class assignments. Eventually, I let go of what she said because I didn't have another choice. I could choose to be miserable and upset being around her, or I could choose joy regardless of what had happened in the past.

I have some extraordinarily fun memories with Sabrina in high school. She wasn't ever going to be my best friend again and that was fine, but eventually, those words she said to me in the middle of my sister's musical were no longer ringing in my ear.

Learning what it looks like to carry grief and joy simultaneously is a funny thing to learn in 7th grade. Gosh, the scales were threatening to leave me in grief of so much brokenness that year, but I clung to my childlike faith that God was who He said He was, and I would feel the scales tipping ever so slightly back to joy one day. Trusting God became an active choice, a choice I would have to learn to make daily.

———

In March of 2022, my mom found out she had breast cancer. I had taken three days of PTO to pretend like spring break was still a thing in the adult world and went home to see my family. It felt like something was a bit off the whole trip, but I attributed it to being the first time I'd ever brought a boyfriend home to meet my family.

I headed back to Nashville and went to work after our trip came to an end. When I got home, my dad called me. I picked up, but he didn't sound like himself. I don't really remember much of the conversation after he said the words, "Mom found out she has breast cancer."

I didn't know what to do after I hung up the phone. One of my college best friends, Sarah, was in town for the night, and she was going to be at my house in three minutes. She could tell something was wrong when she got there, and I repeated back to her what I'd just heard. Sarah's mom had recently walked through a similar diagnosis and so she comforted me in a way not all of my friends could. In a moment of such grief, I was able to be with a friend who knew me and the pain of this situation so well. The Lord orchestrated us being together at this very moment for this very reason and that will never be lost on me.

Mom quickly had surgery and we hoped and prayed that was all she would need, but we were then told she would need chemo and radiation. We felt devastated, but ready to power through this and were beyond grateful that the cancer had not spread.

As the treatments began that summer, I was struck with a new fear in the one place I thought I could be safe: my home. Many attempted break-ins happened all around our home, and there was even an incident where someone broke into my car, stole my garage opener, and entered our garage in the middle of the night.

Like I talked about earlier, I didn't sleep through the night after that summer of attempted break-ins for a really long time. Even when I started sleeping again, it only happened in spurts. A year later was the first time that I can remember getting quality sleep most nights.

That fall, more heartbreak struck. My entire department at work quit in just two months leaving me as the last man standing, and on top of that, our eight-year-old dog passed away unexpectedly. At this point, I was numb. I wasn't mad at God; I just wasn't sure I trusted Him or wanted to talk.

I am an avid journaler and need to get my feelings on paper daily. Typically, I go through a few journals a year, but I didn't make it through one single journal in 2022. My lack of trust in God played out in my relationships and friendships too. Would they leave as well? Would those parts of my life break and fracture like everything else? I grasped on as tight as I could, suffocating the life out of several people in my life, leaving them exhausted too.

In March 2023, I found myself walking around the Colosseum in Rome, Italy, taking in its splendor. It was once a place of gathering for entertainment– entertainment at the cost of people's and animals' well-being and lives– but now it is crumbling ruins. Beautiful but sad. I've seen dozens of pictures throughout my life of the Colosseum, but hearing about the Colosseum's history from a local while standing inside of this amphitheater was another thing altogether.

I looked around thinking that my life felt like it had been deteriorating like this Colosseum over the past year. It felt far beyond repair, better off as a historic site than a functional structure.

But I kept clinging to this verse:

"Therefore do not be anxious about tomorrow, for tomorrow will be anxious for itself. Sufficient for the day is its own trouble."   *– Matthew 6:34*

I can't change some of my circumstances, but I can change my perspective. I tend to leave no room for God to work and don't easily trust that He is working and doesn't need me intervening.

When my relationship ended and my job felt unbearable in the spring of 2023, I was at the end of myself. I felt as if the majority of what was good in my life had been stripped from me in the past year, but I returned from this trip with my family ready for a fresh start, and felt a shift. God placed two incredible Bible studies at my feet for me to join. I got more serious about spending daily time with the Lord and finding ways to think and serve others more than myself.

It's easy to get caught up in me, me, me, but I want to serve God and love Him more, and through that, love others more too. I started writing and naming off all that I am grateful for daily and that shifted something in my heart. I found a new church, one that I deeply connected with and found community with. A place that I looked forward to getting up and going to each Sunday.

I quit my job at the addiction treatment center. It felt like the weight of the world was on my shoulders. God plopped the opportunity of a lifetime into my lap: a little yellow house that helps people called Daystar.

I spent more time with old friends and invested in some new friendships too. I found myself with more free time than I had had in years, and I decided I didn't want to waste one more second.

Throughout that year of so much pain, I did have good moments, but they felt deeply overshadowed by the darkness I felt. I don't remember much of that year besides the few big situations I mentioned. The lack of sleep and inability to express how much all of this had affected me left me numbing what was left.

But the light is coming, I know it. I feel it. I've felt the scales tilting back toward joy instead of sadness. I've seen the scales removed from my eyes, like Paul did in Acts, seeing God for who He is, seeing my life for what it is. Some days are better than others, but it's an active choice I get to make about how I want to view my life.

I've always had to dig deep to find joy in grief and to trust God and what He's doing, maybe a little more than the average person, but I want to see God for who He is: a kind, gracious, loving Father who is refining me in moments that hurt like crazy and maybe I'll never understand why they were necessary, but I've seen time and time again that I'm never more filled up than I am when I'm abiding in Him.

In one of my Bible studies, we're going through a study in 1 and 2 Chronicles. The other day we were talking about 1 Chronicles 16 where David gives a song of thanks. David's praise wasn't about himself, it was about God. His heart was in the right place. My praise has to be centered on God instead of myself.

David had a mindset of abundance instead of scarcity. He named all the ways God had blessed them, not all the ways God could serve them. A lot of times I find my prayers to be about how I want God to further enrich my life. I don't take the time to simply thank God with no further requests.

The thing about praise is it may not change your situation, but it certainly will change your heart.

It's always been wild to me that Jesus had all of the answers, yet He still wept (John 11:35). In my morning devotional the other day, it was talking about that very verse. And then it said this, "Jesus had all the answers, and He still wept... Maybe **not** understanding is what grows our faith. Maybe being too full of answers is what slows our faith."[17]

Jesus wept for his friend. He knew his friend would die but would rise again, yet He still wept. Jesus could identify with others in their sorrow. He had all of the answers. He knew what would happen to Lazarus. Yet He wept.

Have you ever read the end of a book before you even begin it? I once did when I was reading *Harry Potter and the Half-Blood Prince*. My parents and I went to Walmart the day after it was released and picked up my very own bright and shiny copy of this newest book in the Harry Potter series. But my third-grade self was exhausted from waiting to find out what would happen next. Y'all know how long those books are. So I skipped ahead to the very end, and I quickly wished I hadn't. I didn't have a single desire to finish the book after knowing how it all would end.

Knowing the ending of this story, my story is exactly what I want. I wish God would tell me how my life is going to turn out, where I'm going to live, who I'm going to be surrounded by, and what I'll be doing. But if I knew, would I be as interested in the messy in-between that gets me to those places?

I've wept with Jesus this year, but I've also felt my faith expedited in a way that I've never felt before. To be hungry for Jesus and to want to soak up every single word in Scripture, it's something I didn't know I could feel this deeply. And I couldn't have felt it without that messy middle.

What "why" questions are at the forefront of your mind and heart today? We don't have to sugarcoat the hard times, but moving our mindset to one that finds the good and seeks positivity can not only change us but also the people around us.

Life is really hard and good and unexpected and heartbreaking and I'm grateful I get to feel fully alive for all of it. No matter the cost. I want so desperately for this equation of grief and joy to be a balanced one. Grief can exist with joy. Both can be true.

I see Jesus picking up the pieces of the crumbling colosseum I tried to put together for myself. The difference is He is picking up the pieces and making my life *better*. I trust that He won't leave me to be just ruins.

Chapter 12

YESES, NOS, & BOUNDARIES

I lugged behind me a very heavy suitcase and my eyelids wanted so desperately to close and for me to lie down in the middle of the Lisbon airport. I searched all around for a man holding our names on his sign, and finally, I saw him, my new hero. He asked if he could take my bags, and I could not pass them to him quickly enough. Several of my friends and I had flown through the night to get to Portugal. It was the trip that had made it out of the group chat.

For graduate school, I was supposed to study abroad in Austria, but alas, the world shut down in 2020 and instead, we studied abroad online. Yes, **online over Zoom**. But that's a story for a different day.

Two years later, my best friend from grad school, Savannah, texted me a screenshot of an email we had received about a Belmont alumni trip to Portugal. "Should we go?" Sav asked me. Half-kidding, I responded back, "Let's do it."

Next thing I know, four of my friends and I are going on the trip: Sav, Jacob, my yes-man best friend, Ally, my yes-woman best friend, and Madison, one of Sav's good friends and a soon-to-be good friend of mine too. We paid our deposit and headed to Portugal. I didn't think twice about it. I had saved some money for a fun trip and here the fun trip was, right in front of me.

I can't remember many weeks where I laughed as hard as I did that week. We rode around on tuk tuks, ate our body weight in Portuguese custard tarts, met a lot of new friends, and went catamaraning around the coast on an extremely windy and cold day.

As someone who tends to overthink every detail of my life, I usually debate back and forth about a trip or even small moments like going out with friends or what rug to buy for my living room. I'm so focused on being a productive adult that I've lost the joy of play and fun and whim.

I feel like I'm on a mission to reclaim a little piece of the old me.

I don't remember growing up and feeling like I was the kind of kid who needed as much structure as I do now. All I remember is my mom having us play outside all day long when we weren't at school, which bred creativity and the ability to figure out a way to entertain myself at any given moment, something I'm especially grateful for as an adult.

The world has an endless amount of possibilities, especially if you're single, in your 20s. You can live anywhere, be anyone, and spend your time however you'd like. How do we move from being crippled by decisions to allowing ourselves to have fun again?

I want to have unplanned, unexpected moments of yes; yeses to Portugal, or even just yeses to running over to Crumbl Cookies with my neighbor at 9 pm in our pajamas. But I'm struggling to make sense of seeing what yeses are mine to take and what nos I should probably give.

———

Everyone I know is getting married or having a baby. And I mean it. Between New Year's Eve and the end of May, I have seven weddings to go to. Tons of parties are on the docket leading up to celebrating those events, and I'll be headed out of town for a variety of other reasons throughout the next six months. I think I'm left with maybe two weekends in my own bed until June? My gut reaction has been, *maybe I'll skip a few of those weddings*. I've had seasons where I've felt like a stranger in my own city. I don't want that feeling again.

This weekend, I went to Birmingham to visit one of my very best friends in the world, Abby. She is one of the most hysterical people you will ever meet. Upon arrival at her house, the first thing we did was dig through the forest-green garbage can outside, looking for her wallet that she had thrown away, only to find it on the floorboard of her car on our way to dinner.

Dull moments don't exist with Abby.

I came to town for her baby shower. Baby James is due in the next few weeks so this is the last time we get to spend time as just the two of us. I could've missed this weekend with her, but I also could've missed the joy that comes with celebrating my people. It's not every day you're having a baby or committing your life to someone forever and ever more, amen.

We spent the weekend side by side talking about baby clothes and big, huge life changes and when would Auburn ever be good at football again. Our lives look different, yet they're the same in a way.

I could've missed this, but I'm grateful I didn't. I could've been in Nashville with my friends, but I could never have this weekend back with my very best friend.

I feel like deep in my bones I know how much it matters to celebrate people well. In the big moments, in the small moments, it just feels significant. As much as we get bogged down in the negativity going on around us, I feel like we've got to celebrate every little moment we can. At the cost of our time, our resources, our weekends in our own bed. These yeses feel necessary and needed, and I won't pass them up. Say yes to celebrating your people. We were created for such joy-filled moments with our people. These yeses matter to our souls and our friends.

———

After 11 pm in Nashville, some of the traffic lights around my neighborhood change into a yellow flashing light through the night. I always know I'm out past my bedtime when I'm driving along and I see the lights flashing neon yellow at me through every turn.

Before the 1920s, no yellow lights existed on traffic lights, just red and green. You either stopped at the light or you powered through. Without a warning, lights became red leaving no time to slow down or better yet, speed through. Maybe didn't exist, it was black and white (or in this case, green or red).

I feel tugged in a million directions by well-intended advice. Just say yes to everything and live your fullest life! Or set boundaries and say no to what isn't serving you. How do I balance both? Proceeding with caution when the light turns yellow leaves me at a crossroads of a decision I need to make or else I'm about to get hit by oncoming traffic. I can't hesitate; I need to make a decision.

Balancing what's a red light and what's a green light makes me feel like I'm color- blind. How do I know before I get too close to the light? Rarely are decisions made hovering on yellow, yet I toe the line of hitting the gas and slamming on the brakes frequently. Without spending time with God, without my relationship with Him, I am color blind.

I need to be in His Word to know Him more and to hear His voice more clearly. I need conviction and correction from Him in order to know what's a yes or a no, what's a red or green light. Without Him, I'm not sure what color the lights are and what they are trying to signal. Should I stay or should I go? Should I cross this road or do I need to pause for a minute?

Politics and elections bring out some anxiety in me. I've got friends who are liberal, conservative, and everything in between. We all grew up differently when it comes to learning about politics: some had parents who were very into politics, and others couldn't have cared less. As we become adults, this is one of those topics we begin to learn and understand for ourselves.

I do my research on candidates, not wanting to ever blindly vote for a candidate based on what everyone in the world thinks. But this is one of those subjects that I do not ever really care to talk about with people. I have watched so much grief and division come from it, so I don't enjoy talking about it over and over with people.

And don't get me wrong. What I'm not saying is that I'm unwilling to have conversations about issues in our country and what should be done, but there is a difference in discussing issues in our country vs. harping on how much we hate a certain political candidate on either side over and over.

I had a friend during the last presidential election who only wanted to talk about the election and bash all of the candidates she did not agree with. I got so tired of hearing about it, but as a slightly unaware people pleaser, I would listen to her rant and rant and never disagree or agree with her. I would just let her talk.

But I finally hit a point where it was bringing me so much anxiety only talking about this one thing and making it seem life or death if her candidate did not win. One night when she was ranting about the election, I kindly but firmly said to her, "I know this is so important to you and I want to hear about what's important to you, but I also don't feel like I can talk about politics with you anymore. It is bringing out anxiety in me. I hope you can understand, you know how much I love you."

I did not want that to be a subject of conversation anymore, ever, with her. It was draining me and had become the focal point of our friendship.

She was not thrilled about this statement, and it led to our friendship slowly disintegrating. She could not respect the boundary that I set in place, and that boundary was hard for me to make.

That was one of the first moments I felt like, in adulthood, I was standing up for what I needed and setting a boundary that I knew would probably not be received well. It was a small boundary. It wasn't life or death, but for me, it felt big. I did not want this to taint our friendship, but my anxiety can build and build, and sometimes I get to a point that is hard to return from. Especially when it was 2020, the year of the pandemic and a very big presidential election, so it felt necessary.

I know it matters that we talk about important issues and stand up for what we believe in. For me, boundaries create that balance.

———

Someone told me yesterday that a friend of mine was mad at me. That was news to me because everything seemed fine between us. We had just spent a lot of time together the week before! I heard that she was mad about a situation that had happened over a year ago. I immediately picked up the phone and asked if we could talk.

She reluctantly started telling me about the situation and why it made her upset. I asked that if something happens in the future could she come to me as soon as it happens? I was hurt and blindsided that she didn't tell me and instead told my friends. It was a misunderstanding and could have been squashed in the moment a year ago.

In college, that is a moment that I would have let just continue to be a problem because I would have been so upset that they had not told me themselves. And confrontation is hard. I'm working on setting the record straight the moment I receive incorrect information or notice that something may be wrong. It's easy to let things go and fester until they bleed and blister and then I have to take care of a wound that could've been prevented.

In my experience over the past few years, healthy and respectful confrontation has usually left me feeling closer to the person I've had a conflict with because I see that we can overcome roadblocks and our friendship isn't just surface level. I love what author and speaker Mark Groves says about this: "Walls keep everybody out. Boundaries teach people where the door is."[18]

Boundaries used to make me think of a tall wall keeping intruders out and those residing in the boundary are safe but isolated. Over the years, I've learned that boundaries are in place to help us better connect with others and ourselves. Boundaries promote and create accountability rather than preventing access and elevating isolation.

We all have areas in our lives that could benefit from some boundaries. Maybe it's how much time you spend with a boyfriend each week. Maybe you're working 80-hour weeks at work and you feel your mental and physical health declining because of the lack of work-life balance.

For the rest of our lives, we will be working to find the right balance, but what if we actively start seeking out those boundaries today?

My senior year at Auburn, I lived in a tiny three-bed, two-bath house affectionately known as the Tree House with six girls: Abby H., Abby C., Ally, Kaitlyn, and Mary Lee. I shared a room with Ally, a hilarious, full-of-life, down-for-anything, vivacious Auburn local. She loves a good Coke Icee, frequenting Burger King nightly throughout our senior year.

We were friends before sharing a room but had not spent a ton of time together, so when we moved into the same small room together we quickly found out all there is to know about each other.

I found out that Ally is very ambitious when it comes to her alarm clocks. She set about 20 alarms for each morning, starting at 5:30 am some mornings because she "might go to CycleBar" and ending around 9:30 am because, well, she had a 10 am class.

I, on the other hand, am a one-alarm clock kind of girl. Rarely, I might snooze that one alarm, but that is the only one I set regardless. I also don't believe in the alarm sounds Apple offers. I opt for something more peaceful. For about the last eight years of my life, my alarm sound has been "Patience" by The Lumineers.

After a few months of living together, I had come close to pulling every last strand of my hair out because if I heard that Apple alarm ringtone one more time I was going to throw Ally's phone onto train tracks and do cartwheels when a train ran it over, smashing it into a million fractured pieces.

So instead I did what any mature 21-year-old would do, I sarcastically told her she needed to change her alarm clock to a new, less violent alarm sound or else I may never be able to speak to her again.

For a good portion of my life, I have unconsciously tried to implement boundaries, big and small, through sarcasm. That way if it doesn't go over well, I can claim, "It was just a joke!"

I had to dig deep, to kindly and lovingly figure out how to communicate my boundaries to others. When I lived in that tiny house with six girls, I wish I had known how to be more clear and kind with boundaries because Lord knows we needed some.

And as for Ally, she changed her alarm ringtone to "Here Comes The Sun" by The Beatles.

"Here Comes The Sun" came up on my Spotify mix a few days ago, and I immediately skipped. I will never be able to listen to that song again, but at least she honored my request. And I learned a thing or two about figuring out what I need to stay sane.

Boundaries have a negative connotation, but they actually bring fruit to lifeless areas. We need them and so do the people we are surrounded by daily.

I heard research professor and author Brene Brown once tell a story about how she was having a holiday party with her neighborhood friends, and one of these friends was known for drinking too much, getting drunk at a holiday party, and passing out. Brene saw the friend before the party and pulled her aside to tell her how excited she was that her family would be coming to her party. Then, she asked her friend if she could refrain from drinking any alcohol at the party.

The friend laughed and made a joke about her passing out at the last holiday party and promised she wouldn't get that sloppy again. But Brene responded and said that she was asking that she not drink a drop at this party. Brene reinforced how excited she was that their family would be at the party, but the woman wasn't having it and never spoke again to Brene.

About a year later, the woman went to rehab for alcohol.

Brene talked through the different options. Should she just not have alcohol out for anyone at the holiday party? No, she didn't want one person to have that much power and control the party (and Brene is sober!).

Should she have let her drink and not say anything? No, because her kids were watching and she didn't want her children to be around someone drunk at their party.

So, she kindly set a boundary. She wasn't mean. She just stated what was needed. We can control how we approach delicate situations, but we can't control how people react.

Boundaries don't have to be this harsh punishment of us laying down the law. They can be kindness toward yourself and others if you frame it in a way that exudes wanting the best for both parties.

Boundaries are a balancing act. We are all in the process of learning what that looks like for each of us. We have to extend and receive grace when it comes to figuring out what boundaries work for us and those around us. It's hard, but boy, is it worth it.

What I want to be is braver than I feel. I seek the courage to do what is needed whether that's a yes or a no. Whether it's deciding on dinner or figuring out what my next career move is. I want to remember what matters and shed the rest, peeling back new layers of myself until the decisions come easier and easier. It can really be that simple if my overcomplicated mind can find a way to unweave itself like a kid playing Twister. I might be able to get my way out of this mess or maybe I collapse on the floor from exhaustion of holding myself up in shapes I wasn't made for. But I'll begin again, each decision, each twist and turn, piece by piece.

Crossroad 3

WHAT YOU WERE MEANT FOR

I sat across from a teenage girl at work this week who told me six months ago she felt like she had no purpose and didn't want to be alive anymore. Ready to be done with the pain. But then, she learned about this thing called hope. Hope found in herself. Hope found in others.

She met with people who cared about her: doctors, counselors, new friends, and family. They reminded her of her worth until she could believe it for herself.

At only fifteen years old, she embodies what this entire section is about. She is seeking out friends who truly care about her and want to see her succeed. She is figuring out what it looks like to put her worth in something other than the boys at school. She is learning what it looks like to have vulnerable conversations with her family.

She has become a bright beacon of light bursting at the seams when she walks into a room. In and through my eyes, she is the definition of delight. I wish I had her courage at fifteen years old.

Instead, I've learned it over a lot more time, a lot more life. And that's okay too. I hope these words in this section will guide you home to people who love you. I pray this will be a nudge to set yourself up well for the decades to come.

More than anything, I hope you grow in appreciation for who you are and what you're meant for. You're meant for community and love and vulnerability and delight and peace in your circumstances.

You are never too far gone to be used by God to further His Kingdom. You don't have to do it all alone. You weren't meant to. You just have to be here, be alive, be fully alive. We'll figure out the rest along the way, every day.

Chapter 13

FRIENDS – FINDING THEM, KEEPING THEM, AND LETTING THEM GO

MAKING FRIENDS

My high school graduating class was 55 souls that I had known practically since I was born. Making new friends wasn't exactly something I had experience with when I finally graduated and went off to college. I thought it would be easy. My eighteen-year- old self had a date with reality coming very soon.

The first friend I remember making in college was a girl named Mattie. We didn't exactly get off to a picturesque start. Mattie and I had joined the same sorority and rode to our first sorority event together with some other girls. The car ride was about 45 minutes over Lake Martin. We arrived at the event, hopped in the pool, and started talking to the other girls in our pledge class. With 99 of us in the same pledge class, it was hard to keep everyone straight, but I knew I'd at least remember the girls I rode with.

As we sat around the pool, I went and moved over to where Mattie was so I could be with someone I knew. We chatted and then she proceeded to introduce herself to me... she had completely forgotten me even after we had been in the car together on the way to the retreat. That was a humbling moment in my very first week of college.

Turns out, Mattie and I were both Exploratory majors, a.k.a. we had no clue what to do with our lives. We found out that we were in the majority of the same classes, so although she had forgotten me I still wanted to be her friend since we would be spending so much time together.

Mattie was from Texas and didn't really know many people at Auburn either, so we bonded over knowing no one and being in an unfamiliar place. We sat in our classes and evaluated the people who we thought would make good friends. From there, we decided who we wanted to try to convince to be our friend.

Our first target: Sarah, a beautiful blonde from St. Petersburg, Florida, who spoke with such kindness and made everyone feel included. I liked her instantly, and so did Mattie.

I was tired of not having many friends, so one day after class I pulled Sarah aside and told her Mattie and I wanted to be friends with her. She didn't really know anyone either so we planned a lunch together and hit it off. I was now 2/2 finding people who were looking for friends too.

About a month after I got to college, my high school boyfriend and I were on the verge of a breakup. A lot about our lives wasn't lining up anymore, but I wasn't sure what to do. I had become friends with a guy in my dorm who had met my boyfriend before and knew about some of the complications we were having. When I finally got the courage to go through with the breakup, I called my new friend right after and he immediately came upstairs, gave me a big hug, and prayed over me right then and there. I had never had a friend quite like that, who just prayed with and for me in a moment.

His friendship taught me so much about what a community with other believers could look like. I was without a single familiar friend or family member nearby, but he became a friend I could count on in that season of so much turmoil. He taught me what it looks like to show up for others in their most vulnerable moments of life, even when he was still a newer friend of mine. He showed me what it looked like to bring Jesus into the conversation without even meaning to. That's just how much his faith meant to him.

The weekend of the breakup, I was afraid to be alone. So after I hung out with my friend from my dorm for a while, I called Mattie. We still barely knew each other, but I didn't want to be alone and if she thought I was weird, so be it.

Mattie immediately asked me to come meet up with her in our dorm courtyard, brought me some warm coffee and sat and listened to me talk. I didn't have the heart to tell her I had never had coffee in my entire life because the gesture itself meant so much. I tried to slurp down some of the black liquid as I told her what happened.

In author and counselor Debra Fileta's book *Reset,* she discusses how the conversations we have are broken down into three levels: facts, opinions and ideas, and feelings.[19] Facts are conversation starters: where are you from, what do you do for work, do you have siblings, and so on. Opinions and ideas dive a little deeper and that could look like discussing what your thoughts are on anything from who should be president, why summer is your favorite season, or who you want to see be the next lead of *The Bachelor.*

Feelings are the most vulnerable parts of friendship. I sat on that little concrete bench with a girl I barely knew discussing how I felt about my breakup, why I thought it was hard but necessary, and how I still felt sad although it was the right decision.

She didn't make me feel weird or like an oversharer (although in hindsight I might have been). She sat and listened to this stranger who was crying over a cup of black coffee she was barely drinking. I didn't know it then, but Mattie was going to become one of my dearest friends. Someone I would then proceed to be roommates with for two years. Someone who was brilliant and would go on to be an insanely successful engineer. Someone who I would have rap battles and poetry slams with in the middle of the night, and someone who I would convince at the last minute to go to a movie premiere with me 30 minutes before it happened even though she had a huge test the next day.

I let Mattie in to see the best and worst parts of me and in return, she did the same. A lifelong friendship was born in a very weak, low moment for me.

When I started my second semester at Auburn, I had made some friends, but I was still hoping to make more. I made a decision that once a week throughout the entire semester I would ask a stranger to lunch. I asked strangers in my classes, people I met briefly in meetings of organizations that I was a part of, and girls I met in line at Chicken Salad Chick. (If the freshman 15 is real, it's because of that buffalo barclay chicken salad.)

Some of those lunches were vibrant and I immediately connected with the person sitting across the table from me. Others were a little harder to read, and we didn't find much common ground. I loved both types of people because regardless of whether or not we became best friends, I had met somebody that I could smile and wave to as I walked across campus.

Sixteen new friends were made during that second semester of lunches with strangers. I have been a bridesmaid in the weddings of a few of those friends. Two of those new friends I ended up living with my senior year. Another ended up moving to Nashville when I did and every once in a while, we get lunch. Some of those new friends introduced me to other people who I became great friends with. I realized that I wasn't quite as bad at making friends as I thought I was.

When I moved to Nashville after college, I found myself struggling to make friends again. It's a little bit harder to make friends in the real world vs. college. I wasn't constantly around people my age. I had to seek them out. I asked friends to connect me to people they knew in Nashville. I tried to get involved at a church ASAP to get connected with like-minded people. I made great friends, but making friends as an adult is bittersweet because instead of being at the same school for at least four years, these friends could move at any time.

My friends have shifted and changed during my time here. One of my dear friends, Chika, moved away after just a year of such a fun, deep friendship to go to medical school in Oklahoma. I lived with an amazing human named Savannah for 2 years, and we had been best friends in Nashville for 4 years when she moved to Atlanta with her husband. I kept feeling like I was collecting friends who would be for life but might not be in my city forever.

I was in a Bible Study recently and became friends with several of the girls in the group. I was so excited for some new friends and was hoping we'd take our friendships deeper. One girl in particular I thought I'd really hit it off with, and I asked her to hang out one weekend. She was busy, and I was bummed but totally understood.

Then, a few weeks later at church, I saw her and we got to talking and I told her we should grab dinner soon. She then told me that she'd gotten so comfortable just hanging out with her roommates and wasn't branching out much. She told me that hopefully, she'd have more time in the fall to hang out... which was three months away!

My feelings were a little hurt, but she seemed to mean so well. Why didn't she want to hang out with me and make time for just one dinner?

Trying to make friends as an adult is such a vulnerable thing. People get in their rhythms of friendship. I wasn't someone who ever had a tight friend group until I moved to Nashville. Having a group you can always count on to have plans with is such a blessing, but as members of our group have gotten married and moved away, our group has shifted. As I'm writing this, I'm at a place where I have the capacity and the longing for new friendships as well as maintaining the old.

I have a friend whom I love dearly that I hang out with about once every other month. I look at her life on social media and envy the friendships and friend groups she seems to have. I feel so weird as an adult wishing to be a part of a friend group, but it's hard finding the balance between inviting yourself in and letting it happen organically. How do we invite people into our friendships but also maintain the closeness of the ones we have? I find myself coming back to that question over and over as the seasons change.

KEEPING FRIENDS

In 2016, I guess I hadn't had enough of going to unfamiliar places and having to make new friends, so I went to Kanakuk Kamps 15 hours away from my hometown. Again, I knew no one. I pulled up to the camp, nervous and anxious, and had people running toward my car jumping up and down to welcome the counselors and staff in! Can't say that helped my nerves, but I tried to smile and roll with it. They checked me in immediately after I arrived.

During the camp sessions, counselors aren't allowed to have their phones. After they finished checking me in, they asked for my phone and I was so nervous that I handed it over without calling my parents to tell them I had made it to this camp they'd never heard of states over from Georgia.

They really loved me for it.

Anyway, I walked into my living quarters with my belongings. In our space were about 18 bunk beds in the tightest rows you'd ever seen. I don't know if I'm being dramatic, but I genuinely don't remember there being any windows in this building either. I put my stuff down and introduced myself to some of the girls. One of the first girls I met was Kennedy. She had long, auburn hair, loved Beyoncé, and repped Oklahoma State everywhere she went. Go Pokes.

I immediately loved her. About a week into our friendship, I told her she would be a bridesmaid in my wedding one day. She confirmed that I would be in her wedding one day too. When ya know, ya know.

Anyone could tell we were thick as thieves, but I doubted anyone thought our friendship would make it outside of camp. She was at school in Oklahoma; I was in Alabama. She would, without a doubt, be moving back to Texas, and I always knew I'd be in Nashville.

After seven weeks at camp, we were finally done with our time working in the kitchen. It was a sad, stormy last day at camp which felt fitting given the amount of tears Kennedy and I shed saying goodbye to each other.

Seven years ago, we became friends, and we are closer than we've ever been. I visited her at OSU. She visited me one summer when I interned in Nashville. When she moved to Austin after college, I came to visit her new place. Then, for her birthday one year, I surprised her with tickets to the Grand Ole Opry! She got to sport her Texas cowboy boots all over the town and see what Music City was all about.

We make the effort to see each other as often as we can, which is about once every year or two. And we always pick up right back where we started. We send voice memos to each other a couple of times a week. We call each other probably once a month. I would venture to say that we text almost every day. Kennedy is the kind of friend I always dreamed of having. She just gets me.

Our dream throughout our entire friendship has been to go to Napa. When we met at 19 years old it sounded like a very grown-up and adult thing to do, and we were all about it.

I'm here to tell you it's finally happening, seven years after we first talked about it. We're headed to Napa in October. We've covered a lot of ground in our friendship, and we've got a lifetime to go, and I wouldn't mind if it's done with a glass of wine in hand.

If our friendship had ended after camp, no one would have thought twice about it. We all have friends for a season and then friends for life. A lot of times friends like that, in such a camp bubble, can be for a season. But we didn't let it be.

———

I have old friends, friends who have known me in a plethora of stages throughout my life, who almost know me better than I know myself. Three of those friends for me are Emilie, Chelsea, and Nikki. I grew up with them and grew into the person I am now with them. They've seen every shade, every boyfriend, every piece of me. We don't get to see each other much now, but when we do, I feel myself loosen up a little. They know me in a way no one else ever will.

I have friends who are my daily life friends. I talk to them every day, see them every week, and we run in the same circles. One of those people for me is Brooke. Brooke and I lived together for three years, and I couldn't be more grateful for those years living together.

I got home once really late after a breakup, and Brooke had turned on the lamps in my room, filled up a cup of water and put it by my bed, and was waiting for me at the door when I got home to help me with my things and hug me while I cried. I have never had a friend quite like Brooke.

I have yes friends. Those friends that are always down for any adventure. Those people in my life are Ally and Jacob. It doesn't matter what it is, they are coming. Even if that means flying to Portugal. They'll do it, and it'll be 10x more fun because they're there.

I have friends who feel like long-lost sisters. One of those people for me is Kennedy. I have a biological sister, Cameron, and I feel lucky to have her in the best friend bucket too. It's a really sweet gift to have a sister who's also your friend.

I have all different types of friends. The sad and fun part of friendships is that you are never done making friends. You are never finished growing and nourishing your friendships.

LETTING FRIENDS GO

Making new friends at Auburn was exciting and thrilling for a small-town gal like me. Who knew there could be so many options when it came to friends? Some of my new friends came from big cities and knew lots of people at Auburn from their hometown. I became friends with a gorgeous, adventurous girl named Ann. She had tons of friends already and had lots of connections at Auburn. I felt honored in a way to be her friend.

Throughout college, we were together for lots of big moments for one another. There were a few moments that felt lopsided, like she only wanted to hang out with me when it was convenient, but there was a moment of real vulnerability when she confessed that to me and it brought us closer. We met up for breakfast often and confided in one another about so much of life.

After graduation, we kept in touch with one another. We were in different cities, but we talked and texted often enough that it felt like our friendship was going to make it. She came to visit one weekend and it felt different. Lots of gossip, talking bad about some of our old friends, and seeking out the next best option for everything. It deeply pained me because this was a friendship I wanted to see go the distance, but I felt a little sick after our interaction like I needed to be someone else to be her friend.

We didn't have a moment to tell each other that the friendship was over, but I didn't reach back out to her much after that weekend, and she never reached back out either. I felt a silent confirmation that this friendship was coming to a close, and with no further communication, it seemed like she felt that way too.

It hurt me deeply, and some days it still does. Seeing her posts on social media and not knowing much about what's going on in her life feels wrong, but I know we had different needs in our friendship that we couldn't give to each other anymore.

Friend breakups are sometimes more painful than relationship breakups. Some friend breakups happen slowly over time, fading out without any other reason than we both have grown and changed and that's led us to different places. Some friend breakups happen suddenly when one life event shatters what reality once was or someone pushes you to choose to not have them in your life anymore.

Losing friends is hard, messy and painful. Sure, it makes room for something or someone new, but having a history together and then silently calling quits on a friendship feels like a betrayal. We talk about relationship breakups, but no one prepares you for how hard it is to lose a friend in your 20s.

LOVE YOUR NEIGHBOR

When I didn't move back home post-college, I looked to friends in my new city to become my extended family. I needed people who I could be with when work left me on empty or when a date went wonderfully well or wonderfully awful. We weren't meant to do this all alone.

I wish we still lived in a time where we could trust that we were safe enough to leave our doors unlocked and people could drop by whenever. Maybe we can't do that anymore, but we can create space in our lives to show up for our people. Your new friend just lost her mom? Bake her a casserole and leave it on her porch. Your best friend is missing home? Bring some home to her and invite her and her people over for a picnic in your backyard.

Instead of asking people to let me know what they need, I want to be better about showing up with what I've got: a listening ear or dinner or coffee. Even if it's not convenient. That's how we're going to find and keep the friends we want in our lives. I want that in my city I'm now claiming as my home. Your city is only as good as your people are.

I grew up in a little house on Sutton Road from the time I was born until I was eleven years old. We lived next door to two fun girls, Bailey and Lindsey, who were around my sister's and my age. We played together for what felt like every single day after school, making up stories and dreaming big dreams and talking on our silver and purple walkie-talkies, (if you're a real one you remember ChatNows) and roller skating down our driveways.

Bailey and Lindsey were like bonus sisters to us, we saw them just about every hour we weren't in school and ran all around our backyard turning it into faraway lands through the stories we would make up and create.

Then, my family moved into a house a few miles down the road from Bailey and Lindsey, in that cul-de-sac that shaped my life. We still saw them often but were sad to not be next door to our friends anymore.

I think God knew we loved having neighbors our age and we were really lucky to have new neighbors that were also the same age as Cameron and me: Rachael and Heather. We played together all the time too, jumping in and out of Rachael and Heather's pool, jet skiing, and tubing all around the little pond in our backyard, sometimes even carpooling to and from school together.

When I moved off to college, after a few months in Auburn I knocked on the door of my dorm neighbor and asked her if she wanted to play a game on the Wii with me in my dorm room. We became such close friends and a lot of my college memories have this sassy, fiery Colombian girl named Amy wrapped up in them.

I've never known a life without my neighbors playing a big role in the story unfolding around me.

I couldn't wait to meet my neighbors when I moved to Nashville. Real-life adult neighbors! My parents and I pulled up to the house my friends and I were renting on a corner lot in 12 South and I saw my neighbor getting into his car. I immediately jumped out of my car filled with every last one of my belongings and started waving! He looked at me like I was a crazy person, got in his car and started driving away.

I was totally disappointed that this was my first interaction not only in my new city but also with my new neighbors. I still held out hope though for the neighbors across the street. I bet they would be as excited to meet me as I was them.

I was wrong. Well, except for sweet William, a kind soul who I often passed leaving for the night shift at work when I was getting home from night grad school classes. He was always so kind to me.

When I moved into my new apartment a few weeks ago, I wanted things to be different. I wanted to know my neighbors. It feels weird living in a world where we pass by strangers on the street without making eye contact or saying hello. I'm no Martha Stewart, but I finally whipped up some courage and cookies, wrote notes to my new neighbors, and left them at their doorsteps. I wanted them to know they could always call or text or knock on my door if they needed anything. That's what neighbors are supposed to be there for!

Along the way, I'm worried that we have lost the art of living out what being a neighbor, in a physical and spiritual sense, means. God has put you and me in the homes we've lived in for a reason. He has placed us in the jobs, relationships and friendships we have for a purpose. I don't want to miss out on the people right in front of me. Even if I don't become best friends with my next-door neighbor, I still want to be in their corner and them in mine.

Making friends takes courage. Keeping friends requires persistence. Letting friends go creates room for God to bring the right people in. Love the people right in front of you while you can. Loving those around you is always, always, always worth it.

Chapter 14

DATING IN A DIGITAL WORLD

accidentally became a professional matchmaker over the course of 24 hours. I didn't mean to. I used to joke about becoming a matchmaker and as a loyal *The Bachelor* fan for years, I've always wanted to create my own version of this famous reality TV show... except maybe a little more wholesome?

I know so many incredible single people, and one day I thought I'd just start a spreadsheet of all the friends I had that were interested in being set up. I had friends fill out a form with some basic info and the kind of person they were looking for... and that was pretty much it. It became this funny joke. Maybe I could set a few friends up and make my matchmaking dreams come true.

But then I started seeing names on my spreadsheet that I didn't know. It didn't bother me, it just made me laugh that somehow this Google Form had gotten around to random people. A lightbulb went off. Why not expand my services to my whole social circle?

I posted the link to my matchmaking questionnaire on my Instagram story, and after 24 hours, I had 80+ signups of people looking for love. I received texts and hundreds of DM's about what I was doing. Everyone and their mother (literally, I had people's moms reaching out) wanted me to help them find love either for themselves or someone they knew!

This was not at all the response I was expecting. But I don't do anything halfway, and by the end of the first week of my matchmaking fun, I had set up 40+ people on dates. I had gotten out of a relationship a handful of months before and was still a little sad about it, but something about helping other people find potential love made me the happiest I had felt in a long time. I laughed and laughed over some of the submissions. I couldn't believe the things people had entrusted me with: their political beliefs, very, VERY detailed responses about the kind of person they were looking for, their religious beliefs or the lack thereof, and so much more.

I felt honored to be trusted with this information and that friends and acquaintances of mine were trusting me to set them up. I had just started a new full-time job and had stumbled into matchmaking all at the same time, so I started spending all of my free time outside of work matching couples. Some people didn't believe me when I reached out to them (shoutout to their mischievous friends for signing them up without them knowing), and a few were shocked I had followed through on finding someone to go on a date with them.

Dates were planned, and people started going out. The messages started flooding in about their dates. One girl said it was the first date she had ever been on with a Christian, and she was so thankful. Another guy told me after his date that he had so much fun… but he had just gotten out of a relationship a few weeks before and realized he was not quite ready for a new relationship.

That might have been helpful information before I matched him, but I digress.

I was encouraged by people's willingness to be set up blindly, but I was discouraged by people who looked up their matches on social media and then proceeded to say they weren't interested. More times than I wish I could count, a guy would respond back and say the girl wasn't his type and refuse the date. Why miss out on an opportunity to get to know someone new who has a lot of the same interests as you? I felt hurt by their comments about other people. I wanted to jump through my phone and yell at them, but I was able to wrangle in my Enneagram 8 self. If I found someone that met the qualifications you're looking for, how do you know you don't want to go out with them?

It has been an all-over-the-place experience. As I'm writing this, we're a few months into matchmaking and I've had 300+ responses to my matchmaking form. People from all over the country are looking for love from Boston to Dallas and everywhere in between.

When did dating get so complicated? Many submissions said they had never been on a date before.

Others weren't sure how to ask a girl on a date or what they should do for a date. I felt like I was doing a case study on dating in the 21st century.

I am a part of the generation that is the first to grow up with phones in our hands. I remember getting Facebook in 7th grade. Several of my friends already had Facebook, and I was thrilled to be joining the elite group that would be on this little app. I would scour through it daily, seeing who was in a relationship with whom, who had broken up, and all the other things we used to post all over social media.

We've grown up with endless options when it comes to how to meet new people. We can meet someone online from the other side of the country without ever leaving our house. It's kind of wild and exciting and also weird. Before, you dated people who were in your circle, whether through mutual friends, at a bar in your hometown, or in your class at college. Now, you can download an app and meet someone hundreds of miles away from you or across the street from you; the world is your oyster.

The first time I downloaded a dating app, I was beyond terrified and embarrassed to make my profile, so I left it to be created in the hands of my friends as we were eating chicken tacos at Red Headed Stranger. They handed my phone back to me, and I looked through my profile. I cringed a bit, but whatever. Might as well see what happens, go on a date and have a free meal, and at least get a good story out of this.

Having strangers message me freaked me out a little, so it took some getting used to. A lot of the conversations were really shallow, and I started not enjoying it at all.

After a few weeks, I thought about deleting it altogether until I saw a profile that piqued my interest. Christian guy, cute, seemed normal... but it looked like he didn't live in Nashville? Didn't understand how that could be possible since I set my profile for Nashville, but what did I know? I'm a dating app novice after all. I gave his profile a like and then moved on with my life, forgetting about him pretty quickly.

Jake then messaged me, and we started a conversation. He said that he didn't live in Nashville and wasn't sure if that would be a dealbreaker for me. I didn't think the conversation would go anywhere, so I said that it didn't matter. I was pleasantly surprised at the depth of the conversation, and he quickly asked if he could get my number and call me sometime. I almost didn't respond... a stranger wanting to call me? But my friends said that I had nothing to lose, he didn't live here anyway.

So we talked on the phone for over an hour and then talked a few more times before he came up to Nashville to take me on a date. And then we proceeded to date for a year and a half.

The relationship didn't work out, but I was encouraged that there were people that I could be interested in on dating apps. I never expected to meet someone that I might date long-term on an app, much less work on the very first try. All because of an app, I became a better person through knowing this guy who originally was just on the other side of a screen. He's not someone I would have ever met in the "real world." Our paths more than likely never crossed.

Dating apps have a bad reputation. I get it. I think they're worth a shot if you've got good intentions; chances are you might meet someone… you just never know! Not all dating apps are created equal; however, it's important to talk with friends and do research before jumping into dating apps blindly.

While we were dating, so many friends would say to me, "Oh, that's so awesome that y'all met on a dating app, but I could never do that." Or, my personal favorite, "I just would never want my story to be that I met my future husband on a dating app."

Like hello? People, c'mon.

Those statements would sting a little, but I don't really care how I meet whoever I'm dating as long as I meet them… you know what I mean? I'm not going to let pride get in the way of my happiness, so if we met through a dating app, so be it.

I was listening to a podcast the other day and a relationship coach said she did a poll with Christians in relationships/married, and 33% met their significant other on a dating app, 33% met at a church event, and 33% met through friends and family.

It's kind of a scary stat, I know. But if you want to be married, why not give a dating app a shot for a month? Don't make an idol out of it. Check it once or twice a day, and move on with your life. It feels like a game scrolling through all of the options, but don't let it be that way. Treat it as an evaluation process of who could be right or wrong for you. It's similar to walking into a coffee shop or to church and scanning the room. You unconsciously (or maybe consciously, who am I to judge) look around to see who's in the room. Just like you scan a room you walk into, scan through the dating app profiles. And don't just write someone off because you don't like a guy's shirt or they aren't 6'5. And I feel the need to say:

1. Clothing can be changed; personality cannot.

2. Only 14.5% of men in America are over 6 feet tall.[20] It's tough to hear, I know.

One of my mentors told me to go on three dates with a guy before ruling them out. Unless they are just absolutely unbearable or strange, going with someone on three dates allows you to get past the awkwardness of getting to know a stranger. You can then see what they are really like past the basic get-to-know-you questions.

My mentor had a friend who went on two dates with this guy, and as she got ready for the third date she thought she was about to call off dating him… next thing you know, she's married to this guy.

You will find people that still see dating apps as this taboo, foreign concept that should be left alone and never used, but in reality, dating apps are another tool for you to use as you seek to meet someone to date. Vetting people through social media and mutual friends, if you have any, is a safe bet to make sure you are safe as you date.

Don't invest all of your time and heart into meeting someone on an app. It can and will drain you by scrolling through various faces and deciding whether they are a yes or no, so limit the time you spend on dating apps. Some dating apps have deal-breaker questions as well, so if you know you only want to go on dates with someone who's a Christian or wants kids, that also helps you weed out those who do not share similar lifestyles, goals, or beliefs with you. Depending on where you live, a certain dating app may be more popular than another, so talk with your friends and community to see what might be the best fit when giving dating apps a try.

I felt really weirded out by the fact that I would probably see people I knew on a dating app when I first downloaded one, but I promise it's only as weird as you make it. No one actually cares. You are all on there in hopes of meeting someone, so let that fear go too.

———

When you pick up your phone and click on Facebook or Instagram, you tend to see every happy moment of all 1,000 of your closest friends' relationships. Or maybe you see a picture of a guy you had a crush on in college and wonder what it would be like if you had ended up with him.

Social media has put us into a headspace where everything has to be curated to perfection. Your boyfriend has to be the perfect content for your feed and so does every piece of your relationship that you post. And when it's not going so well behind the scenes, well then maybe you start to doubt that this is the right person for you.

I was talking recently with the gal who does my eyebrows (thank you for your service on these ferocious brows I've got) and we were talking about how hard the dating scene in Nashville feels.

She told me she had been engaged two years ago but broke it off because she thought she might be able to find someone better. "Since then, though, the boyfriends I've had have never compared to him. I'm not sure if I should have broken it off with him now. The grass isn't always greener on the other side, that's for sure," she said to me as she ripped off the gooey wax on my brow.

I've felt that way in relationships too. Could I do better? Every day options appear all around us online. We see curated perfection around us and expect to have a perfect person in our lives regardless of whether or not we are the perfect person.

Maybe you started dating someone who is not at all what you pictured when you thought about who you would date one day. Maybe they are nothing like who your friends date. Why are we so worried about what everyone else expects of us and wants for themselves? We want and need our friends' opinions, but we also have to decide what their and our expectations are.

I've been so selfish at times in relationships, wanting it to be all about me when in reality it needed to be all about Jesus. How was my relationship glorifying Him? Had I made my relationship an idol?

The thing about idols is an idol will reorient society around itself. If you make an idol out of a boyfriend, everything else in your life falls second. Your friendships, your relationship with Jesus, your family, everything.

If you make an idol out of your job, then you work around the clock, always think about work even when you're off the clock or on vacation, and work 80-hour weeks. But when the relationship ends or you get let go from your job, your identity is rooted in something that was sinking sand.

Matthew 7:24-27 says, *"Everyone then who hears these words of mine and does them will be like a wise man who built his house on the rock. And the rain fell, and the floods came, and the winds blew and beat on that house, but it did not fall, because it had been founded on the rock. And everyone who hears these words of mine and does not do them will be like a foolish man who built his house on the sand. And the rain fell, and the floods came, and the winds blew and beat against that house, and it fell, and great was the fall of it."*

Building our lives around what social media fills our heads with leads to unrealistic expectations of what a relationship should be. Placing it on the pedestal of our lives is no place for it to be anyway.

The person you're dating has a few quirks that drive you a little crazy? They aren't the most outgoing person in the room or they don't fold their laundry and put it away immediately? They aren't taking you on extravagant trips or maybe they're already going bald at 25?

But do they love Jesus and are committed to chasing after Him for their entire life? Do you enjoy spending time with them?

Drop what you think "your type" is and your checklist of must-haves that run a mile long. (I'm mostly talking to myself, but you're welcome to take or leave my advice too.) I regret the ways I wanted to pressure past boyfriends into being who I wanted them to be and didn't instead just enjoy their company and love them for who they are.

I once dated a guy with whom I had vastly different beliefs, but I enjoyed his company so much that I decided to look past it. We believed some of the same things, but we did not agree on things that really mattered to me in my faith and vice versa. We would have conversations on a loop about what we believed and tried to convince each other why we were right.

When the most important things to you are not the most important things to who you're dating, it leads to a tough, stressful relationship. And I'm not talking about whether they love Auburn football as much as you or if they are fans of Taylor Swift. If your faith is the centerpiece of your life and it's just a sliver of what they care about, don't cling to them just because you are tired of being alone. God has more for you in your singleness than He does in a dysfunctional relationship. It's better to be lonely and single than lonely in a relationship.

And you know what? Give the guy who's the same height as you a chance. Maybe you actually do love your best guy friend after all. Who cares if you met on Hinge? Leave room for unexpected opportunities; you never know who or what might come your way.

Chapter 15

SINGLENESS IN YOUR TWENTIES

Have you ever landed a book deal and gone through a breakup in the same week? Just me?

On a random Tuesday in February 2022, I received an email while I was at work that hope*books loved my book idea submission and would like to publish my book. I sat in awe at work. I was the only person in my office that day, so I didn't have anyone to tell. I finally collected myself and called my boyfriend. He was so excited for me and couldn't believe that the dream that I had been telling him about throughout our entire relationship was finally happening.

One dream came to life and another dream collapsed later that week. Just like that, on a Sunday afternoon, our relationship ended. We were living in different cities and it looked like that wouldn't be changing any time soon. Long distance was draining us both, and we decided it was best to go our separate ways. It was really hard because we wanted it to work, but situationally, it wasn't making sense anymore, at least for the time being.

At Auburn, I knew many, many people who got engaged while we were still in college. It didn't bother me that much then because I always knew I wanted to move to Nashville, and I had a feeling I'd meet someone up there. I could have never anticipated dating and meeting people could be so hard in a big city. I was single in Nashville for two years before I started dating someone, so when I found myself single again I dreaded knowing I'd have to get back to the Nashville dating scene. It would take some time to heal and move on from my relationship, but now so much in my head has changed.

I had mapped out the life I was going to have with this person. I'd be married soon, kids in a few years, where we would live, what we would do… and now I was single. My friends around me were getting married and having babies, and I felt so alone.

A lot of times I hope to wrap up a story and tie a nice little bow on it, especially in a book like this, but I can't do that with this breakup. I don't fully understand why God allowed it to happen and why He didn't bring us back together when that's what I wanted.

I haven't seen the silver lining fully yet, and maybe you haven't either. The pain of a breakup feels like someone rubbing sandpaper over your raw skin over and over again. I think healing has come in waves, and as I'm writing this, the breakup happened five months ago and I'm having a rough day. It feels so vulnerable, but why is it hard to talk about the desires we have embedded deep into our hearts?

After the breakup, my mentor Kate sent me a beautiful, touching email that I will never forget. She first met me when I was single, saw me through all stages of this relationship and was now seeing me in the grief of something I didn't think would have an end.

One of the best parts of her email to me was this: "He either is your person or he isn't. I don't really believe in soulmates. I think there are multiple people we could make it work with for a loving, lasting marriage. God has the answers, and you will see His hand in your love life all along."

No one has the exact, perfect answer on how your life is going to turn out. You've either met the person you're going to end up with or you haven't. You're either going to get the job or you're not. You may move to LA or you won't, but God's hand is guiding you toward His best. It may lead you back to the familiar or it may take you somewhere new. My need for concrete answers is only making things harder on and for myself.

I didn't expect that this was what my life would look like at 26. But I also wouldn't have believed I'd have a book deal. I certainly didn't think I'd have a job that I loved with my whole heart and treated me so well. I didn't know I'd live in the same city as my sister.

I think I know how I want my story to end, and if I wasn't working on trusting the Lord's timing, I would be figuring out a way to narrate and negotiate this story into being what I wanted.

I heard someone say on a podcast once that the best way to heal from a breakup is to do something that makes you think about someone other than yourself. I took that to heart and started thinking about ways I could do just that.

I signed up to be a childcare volunteer for a nonprofit serving teen moms and showed up the first time and ran around for a couple of hours playing soccer, football, basketball, and just about every sport in between with a five-year-old boy. He had more energy for those two hours than I had in two weeks, so by the end of our time playing together, I was ready for a long bath and bed. I felt so overcome with emotion playing with this little guy, though. The kindness of children always surprises me. They rarely meet a stranger, and they jump right in with whoever is around. It was such a small opportunity to help with childcare for a few hours, but it reminded me that with so much going on in the world and while my breakup hurt, who I am is not tied up in a relationship, or lack thereof.

I have found myself, at times, resenting my friends who are married. They don't know what it's like trying to date out here (and sometimes they even say they can't imagine what it would be like to date at our age... words meant to comfort but burn slightly), but I am really working on giving my friends the benefit of the doubt.

I do know this: We need to have friends that are in every stage of life: single, dating, and married. We all have something to learn from one another and it matters that we're intentional about not excluding people based on their relationship status. I sometimes consciously and unconsciously do that. We often want to be around people that "get it." We can have space for that too, but I don't want to look around and see only people that are in just the exact stage of life as me at all times. We miss out on some really incredible, important friendships if we do that.

———

Here's the phrase I hate the most: "Singleness is such a gift!"

Maybe so, BUT STOP TELLING ME THAT! I roll my eyes so hard into the back of my head that I fear they may get lost back there. I know I have free time that I'll never have again, but I don't want to hear those uttered anymore.

What I dread most is going to weddings alone. My best friend recently got married, and almost all of the bridal party had husbands or boyfriends. I was beyond excited about the wedding, but I hated the thought of being at the reception surrounded by husbands and boyfriends at our table and me being alone.

Being at events like that is weird at times because one of the first questions people ask is if you're dating someone and if you say no… Well, then you're given a bit of a pitiful look, followed by, "I'm sure you'll meet someone soon!" Well, great. Do you want to help me find that person?

I'm learning how to be content in singleness when the world around me is screaming that life is complete once you are married. I know that isn't true. Jesus lived a fully lived life, and he was a single man. How do I live my life being content and also want to be married and meet someone? How do we hold both at the same time?

Social media has also created this weird, almost intrusive lens into our personal lives, especially when it comes to relationships. When I went through a breakup earlier this year, I told my close friends and family almost immediately. As I carried on with my normal life, I was taken aback by how many people would ask me about my relationship... how'd they even know I was dating someone? They knew I had a boyfriend because of social media, but they didn't know we had broken up because, shocking to no one, I was not shouting that from the rooftops online.

That experience has given me a dose of the value of keeping my life a little more private. Once we share a moment or memory with everyone on social media, it no longer is a moment between us and whoever we share that moment with. It becomes a moment, a relationship, that everyone is a part of.

Breakups in your 20s are hard. We are at the age where we could get married if we wanted to, and with each relationship, we're hoping this could be the right person. Walking through this breakup currently is painful, but it is teaching me more about the character of Christ. He is patient with me in my shortcomings, in my doubts of His goodness, so I will be patient with Him as He refines me through the pain of losing someone I care so deeply about. If I can try to embrace the unknown, I have to believe there will be beauty on the other side.

I don't have the perfect solution. I wish I had all of the answers when it comes to hoping for a relationship but not seeing one come to fruition. But I do know this: God didn't intend for us to go through life alone.

Bring your friends into the conversation: your single, dating, and married friends. All of them. I bet they all share disappointments in different ways when it comes to relationships or the lack thereof. Bring God into the conversation. Talk to Him. He cares about your hopes for a relationship.

Married friends, what if you and your husband keep a running list in your Notes app of your friends who are single and then see who you could set up over time? Friends that are actively looking out for you and trying to set you up with people they know are the best kinds of friends. I don't know if you know how much that means to your single friends, seriously.

Checking in with your friends that are in relationships but not married yet also means the world. I crave hearing my married friends' thoughts on frustrations I'm having in a relationship, and hearing their experiences makes me feel less alone. Vulnerability breeds vulnerability and I think there's a misconception that marriage = a perfect life.

Honesty cultivates humility, and humility builds hope. Even if it's a little sliver so you know that you are not alone. I know God is working for our greatest good, whether you're single, dating, engaged, or married. He knows our hearts, and He has not and will not forsake us.

Chapter 16

FINANCES AND GIVING BACK

My dad is one of the smartest people I know. He would tell you he had a hard time in school growing up. Learning was a bit more difficult for him for various reasons, and his school lacked resources to help those who needed specific assistance. That is until Mrs. Barbara came along.

Mrs. Barbara was not pleased with the ways people had labeled my dad and had not assisted him. Dad wasn't sure what he would do when he graduated from high school, and some of his teachers had not been that encouraging about his future because he struggled in school. But Mrs. Barbara was bound and determined not to let him be directionless.

One Saturday morning, she went over to my grandparents' house, got my dad out of bed, and took him over to her house. She had noticed my dad had an interest in landscaping, and she had enlisted the help of her husband to teach him the ropes.

It wasn't long before Dad began his own landscaping business. "Yards by Scott" was where it all began. Then in his early 20s, he started his own business doing golf course construction.

He learned a lot about money and how to invest. Dad knows a lot about everything. (If someone from the History Channel sees this, please have my dad over to the set of one of your shows. He has seen them ALL!)

My dad has a very entrepreneurial spirit, and he started teaching me about money and all of its intricacies at a young age. I can't remember a time in my life when I didn't have a piggy bank. I would slowly drop dimes, nickels, and quarters into my transparent piggy bank and watch the coins pile up. When the piggy bank finally got full, my dad and I took it to the bank and opened up a savings account at the ripe old age of 9. I loved the idea of saving. It sounded fun. As I got older and older my dad taught me about a lot of financial lingo I wouldn't have known otherwise: What is a Certificate of Deposit? What are stocks and what should I invest in? How much should I contribute to my 401k?

None of these financial terms would have seemed important if my dad hadn't assured me that they were. I'm grateful for him for many reasons, one being that I have been able to learn about investing young, which will pay off (literally and figuratively) for the rest of my life.

I don't know if you grew up with a dad like mine or were lucky enough to have a personal finance class in school along the way, but if you didn't grow up learning about finances, you aren't behind. We can start moving the needle toward financial security which we will reap the benefits of for years to come and will honor God in the way we seek to make wise choices with all that He has blessed us with.

———

My first "adult" paycheck came on a dreary day in January. I bubbled with excitement thinking about all of the things I could buy. As soon as that check hit my account, I made my way over to the Green Hills Mall. I wanted to make a purchase to remember this monumental moment, but I had no idea what that purchase would be. I glanced over each window display, deciding which store would win me over.

I found myself in a shop called Sundance which had all sorts of beautiful and eclectic clothing, shoes, and jewelry. I looked through the glass display of rings all shining back at me. My eyes stopped on a rectangular-shaped grayish-purple gem. The next thing I knew, I was walking out of the store with this gem glimmering in my hand.

I can tell you what wasn't running through my mind for that first check: budgeting. Or saving. Saving was actually the opposite of what I wanted to do. I wanted to buy a nice meal, stare at the ring on my hand, and get a honey latte from Portland Brew every day of the week.

Living in Nashville, I have several friends who work for Dave Ramsey's company, Ramsey Solutions. I kept hearing about their Financial Peace University class, so I finally decided one day I would take the course and see what I learned (spoiler alert: I had no intentions of giving up my credit card, sorry Dave. I love my cashback bonus too much.) But I was ready to see what else I could learn from them and what all of the hype was about.

In my first class, me and 15 of my newest friends joined on Zoom to learn from a finance guru approved through Ramsey Solutions. I loved him immediately; he was no-nonsense and knew his stuff. He taught us everything from how to pay off debt, invest, give generously, and everything in between. He showed us how to use the EveryDollar app, a budgeting tool, which was beyond user-friendly.

My excuses for not budgeting were over. Before this class, I was the kind of person who avoided checking my bank account because I didn't want to be reminded of the money I'd spent (a lot of money at Anthropologie, people, a lot.) Now I needed to check weekly to make sure I was on track for my monthly budget and allocating where all of my dollars needed to go.

The lesson from our course that stood out to me the most was the lesson on giving generously. I had grown up my whole life knowing about tithing, but I can't say I took it seriously until I got to college and heard an incredible sermon on the importance of tithing.

I tried harder to tithe consistently after that sermon, but it still was a hit or miss. No more excuses were possible now, though, on my budgeting app I could see the exact percent I was giving each month, and it wasn't as much as I had hoped.

I determined what 10% of my income was each month and decided to just set up auto-pay for weekly donations at church so I couldn't make an excuse about why I couldn't or shouldn't give that week. It pained me a little at first, it seemed like a lot of money leaving my bank account, but I knew the importance of giving back what God has graciously given me.

Looking through our bank statements will quickly show us what we prioritize. God wants us to enjoy our lives. But He wants us to give back and be able to give generously, and we can hold both.

Every Sunday when I sit at church, a slide will pass on the screen with what amount our church family has given this year and how much is needed to sustain the life of the church. Almost every time, the actual amount given each week is less than what the church's needed budget is.

I don't know if my friends and I have been fully educated on the importance of giving, and it didn't fully hit me why it mattered until I reached my 20s.

The word "tithing" literally means tenth in Hebrew. When we tithe, we are opening our hands and trusting God with our finances. Sacrificing reminds us that God will meet us in our needs even if this means money is tight for the month. Without tithing, our churches may lack the resources to provide for their members through programming, staffing, being generous in the community, and so much more.

Tithing is not a way to earn your faith or a way to heaven. It's a way for us to be generous with what God has given us, and as we grow older and potentially have more resources to give generously, then we can go above and beyond tithing and give offerings, what we give beyond our tithe. Unless I have a super tight month, I like to set aside a small extra bit of money besides what I give to the church and look for an opportunity throughout the month to be generous. I feel God often presents to me a moment or an organization or person that is in need. Knowing God has given me the resources to provide just a little in that moment is powerful.

I do not know if I would feel the freedom to be so generous without a consistent budget. I now feel more confident in where my money is going monthly and am continually working on not avoiding my finances and instead being an active and smart participant in stewarding the money the Lord provides me with.

As someone who has worked in the nonprofit world for many years, cheerful givers mean the world to me. When I started working in my first nonprofit role, I would announce to my office every time someone donated, even if it was just $10. The fact that people are willing to give up something to give something to others in need is unbelievable to me and I get to witness that every day.

I have been able to witness thousands of women be given the chance to receive affordable addiction treatment because of the generosity of others. I currently watch kids of all ages come into our faith-based nonprofit counseling center every day, some on a sliding scale, who could not afford our services otherwise. It's all because of the generosity of our community.

What are the causes that you care about? Do you care about affordable housing, under-resourced schools or anti-human trafficking causes? Do some research into the nonprofit community in your area and see what good work is taking place around you. What are some needs they have? Maybe they have an Amazon wish list with items needed for their summer day camp for kids in inner-city schools. Maybe you can give $20 to a nonprofit that is helping single moms attend college with assistance from their ministry.

A phrase I hear often in the nonprofit world is that we need people to give generously with their time, talent, and treasure. The world would be such a vastly different place if we all really poured our time, talent, and treasure into just one organization, whether that is the church, a nonprofit, or a ministry. Could you spare an hour twice a month to sort and pack food donations at your local food bank? Could you give $25 a month to them to further their mission of providing food to families who have none? Are you a talented musician? What if you went once a month to write songs with veterans as a form of music therapy?

It's powerful when we rally around each other for a cause that is changing lives in our community.

Giving generously of what we have changes us from the inside out too.

My mom became a volunteer for Court Appointed Special Advocates, also known as CASA, last year. Through her volunteer work, she serves as an advocate for a 12-year-old girl who is in foster care. My mom had some extra time on her hands, and as a former teacher, this felt like the perfect way for her to make a difference in the life of a kid.

Here's what's happened since my mom took on this child's case: she's been placed in a wonderful home with foster parents and foster siblings. She's received tutoring and assistance in school after falling a little behind due to changing schools every single year of her entire life. She's seen my mom consistently show up in her life when things have gone wrong and she had no one else to turn to. She's even gotten to start taking tae-kwon-do lessons and was named Student of the Month at school.

Here's what my mom has received in return: love from a child that is not her own, the joy of focusing on something and someone that has no relation to her, the opportunity to use her skills and voice to change a life, a heart growing in compassion and understanding for a broken justice system and how lives of children are affected greatly by this system. She has given and in turn, she's received more than she could imagine. It was and is never about receiving, but that is the joy that comes with giving. It changes the people who receive your gifts, and it changes you too.

———

For the longest time, I thought a traditional Savings Account was the only way to save, but we've got a lot more options than I was aware of. Within our savings funds, we want to invest in a plethora of options: stocks, CDs, 401k, Roth IRAs, etc.

A bonus? Find out if your employer has any retirement or investment options for you such as a 401k or Roth IRA and see if you're able to match their contributions. For example, if your company will match up to 6% of your paycheck to your 401k, invest 6% into your 401k every month so you receive that match. You are essentially receiving free money just from investing in your 401k. Who wants to miss out on free money?

Make your money work for you. The younger we start investing, the more time the money has to grow. Spend time learning the lingo. I subscribed to Kiplinger's magazine subscription for a year trying to learn all that I can about finances, and it has helped me tremendously. According to a 2023 study, the average American ages 24-39 has $78,396 in debt.[21] That is a scary amount of money, but with the cost of college tuition, the cost of living, and inflation rising, it is not surprising that debt is racking up for our generation.

Another statistic that surprised me is that more than 57% of Americans do not have more than $1000 in their savings account.[22] Saving money is hard, but without a plan in place, it's impossible. Having a savings account we can rely on when unexpected bills pop up is crucial for our financial well-being and peace of mind when crises arise.

Credit cards can leave us with a false reality of how much money we actually have to spend, leaving many of us in debt that takes us by surprise. If you find yourself buying more than you can afford with your credit card, maybe it's time to ditch the credit card.

Money has always been a topic that slightly stresses me out as an adult. I don't want to think about it, but I know it matters. Setting myself up well for my future takes some effort, but I will be grateful one day that I am constantly learning about how to make my money work for me. I want to be a good steward of what I've been given whether that's big or small.

Money is the second most mentioned topic in the Bible, so it's safe to say that God cares about the ways we spend our money. Our culture preaches we need money to have more things to have more happiness, but the Bible preaches the exact opposite. God wants us to be free, but so many of us are slaves to money and what we think it can give us.

The heart behind how you spend and save your money can shift your life a few degrees in a new direction. If we can start trying to take budgeting and tithing seriously in our 20s, our lives will be different because of it when we take our last breath; this I know. God wants us to be free, and financial freedom plays a role in that. It removes a weight from your chest, wondering how you'll be able to afford a new car or rent or groceries for the week.

By embracing a mindset of intentional spending and diligent saving, we pave the way for a future marked by greater peace and freedom. As we prioritize budgeting and tithing in our 20s, we lay the foundation for a life unburdened by financial worries. With each decision to steward our resources wisely, we take a step closer to the abundant life God desires for us, where every breath is breathed in the assurance of His provision and grace.

Chapter 17

VULNERABILITY

Vulnerability as an Enneagram 8 isn't exactly my specialty. I am the queen of making jokes about hardships in my life and staying as busy as I can to not deal with all of my feelings.

I've been reading Brene Brown's *Dare to Lead* book and it's beautiful, but what is one of the first sections of the book called? Thanks for asking; it's called, "Rumbling with Vulnerability."

Can we rumble with something else? Let's rumble with laughter. Let's rumble with tacos. Rumbling with vulnerability? I'm not sure about that one, Brene.

To rumble with vulnerability feels to me like we're sitting on a sinking ship making small talk instead of just jumping overboard and trying to survive while we still can (sounds a little like *Titanic* the more I think about it.)

I'm on the edge of my seat when rumbling with vulnerability. Let's do it super quick, get it over with, and be done. As I read along in Brene's book, I read a line that really drove an arrow through my heart: "All too often our so-called strength comes from fear, not love... How can we give and accept care with strong-back, soft-front compassion, moving past fear into a place of genuine tenderness? I believe it comes about when we can be truly transparent, seeing the world clearly - and letting the world see into us."[23]

I find fear in having soft-front compassion, leaving my heart exposed to the world. Being braver than I feel is uncomfortable. But time and time again, I see that courage is moving in the midst of fear.

When I was living in an unsafe house, I dreaded when the day would grow dark. I didn't want to get into my bed and go to sleep because I knew in a few hours I would be waking up with a jolt of fear.

I made light of it at work and with my friends. I felt so silly that I couldn't sleep through the night and that my health was really suffering from it, so I pretended like it was no big deal. But I was struggling with the effects it was having on me.

I don't want to talk about my feelings. I don't want to cry and I don't want to be seen as weak. I refused to be known as someone needy or struggling, so I just put on a brave face and prayed that the darkness would end.

What I missed is that the darkness will not become light by my own strength. The light glimmers into my and your story when we invite Jesus and our community in and share in our struggles. I struggled for almost a year before I started to realize that our emotions lead our thoughts and mine was being led by an untrusting, fearful version of me. I couldn't trust in my own strength that no one was trying to hurt me, but those I invited in helped me see that there was more to it than my mind, heart, and body could understand.

It was a vulnerable, raw feeling telling the people in my life that I was so scared of the day ending and having to attempt to go to sleep knowing I'd awake in a few hours with fear. I felt silly, but I had to share that to get better, to have people tell me they've been there too and understood. Inviting people in helped me heal, but it took me months to even begin that process. We have to develop vulnerable hearts to become vibrant, whole, healthy people.

————

The biggest, simple dream I have is that I want to have a huge backyard with shady trees and twinkly lights and a long, long wooden table that can seat more people than you could imagine. I want one night a week where everyone in town knows they are invited to my home and we have a modge podge of charcuterie and sides and mesh it into a dinner. We have conversations and laughter with old and new friends. No one feels like an outsider and everyone is welcome at the table that never ends.

Recently, I was at the summer retreat the nonprofit I work for has each year up on a big, beautiful lake in Kentucky. The week I went to visit was the middle school retreat with about thirty 7th and 8th graders. We spent the morning learning about the Samaritan man and how that story relates to our everyday lives and what kindness could look like in middle school.

We then ate some homemade cheesy pizza bites, threw on our swimsuits, and went tubing on the lake.

When we returned, we had a bit of rest time. It was my first and only full day visiting camp, and I really felt weird about going to my room and shutting the door when my time here was so limited. I left my door propped open and hoped someone might walk by and chat with me. I didn't know if anyone would, but I didn't want to close myself off from what the Lord could do during this moment of rest.

Twenty minutes later, a feisty, vivacious middle school girl walked past, looked in my room, and said, "Who are you?" I replied with, "I'm Mary Spencer, who are you?" This began a two-hour discussion with my new friend. She stood in the doorway for a while before I finally asked her if she'd like to come inside and sit down. I asked her how middle school was and if it felt cliquey. Her immediate response was that she wished she could start her own middle school, getting rid of all of the tables and making the cafeteria have one long lunch table so that no one is left out or separated.

I want that too. We won't always get along with every single person. We may not see eye to eye or have a thing in common, but I hope that I grow in compassion, love, and understanding. I pray I learn how to open my ears, heart and hands to those I disagree with. I want that long table at my house where everyone is welcome and people walk in knowing they are in a safe space where they can be themselves.

Hurt people hurt people; we've heard that phrase before, but I've seen over and over that healed people heal people. We're all walking each other home, to our true home with Jesus. He's prepared a room for you and me if we're willing to accept Him into our hearts fully. As we navigate the turbulent current of our 20s and beyond, our courage to be vulnerable will change us from the inside out, leaving us and the people around us better than we found them.

Our lives are full of splendor and wonder and fun and chaos and joy and sadness and sorrow. Our thumbs are green as we plant and sow seeds that we may not see bear fruit for years or even decades to come. If the garden surrounding you isn't alive yet, cling to hope, friend. It's coming, full of life and fruit and flavor.

———

I didn't mean to spill my guts to the cashier at Whole Foods, but as my favorite childhood phrase used often with my sister goes: She started it.

You can find me frequenting the hot bar at Whole Foods as often as I can. It gives me Thanksgiving vibes over and over again. Fill your plate up with a random assortment of deliciousness and enjoy your life.

After eating dinner with a friend at the glorious Whole Foods hot bar, I picked up a few things of fresh fruit to have at work for the week and headed to check out.

Suzanne dazzled me with a smile as she scanned my fruit and rang me up. "I love seeing you smile!" she said to me. "I'm happy to be alive!" I said in response. I don't know why I said that, but I meant it, I really did. My heart felt full of hope, of new possibilities, of so much joy.

"I wish I saw more people your age smiling," Suzanne replied. She then told me that she wished she had learned the secrets to life at my age so she would have smiled more then.

"I wasn't smiling that much six months ago," I told her. "Six months? That's not that long ago!" she said. "A lot can happen in six months," I told Suzanne.

We talked about the highs and lows in life all in the few minutes it took for me to buy my fruit and pay for my purchase. I grabbed my grocery bag and Suzanne said, "It was so nice to meet you."

I left Whole Foods grinning from ear to ear. After a hard day of work, I was still smiling because God had changed so much of who I am months following so much falling apart and I'm so overwhelmed with joy that I can't help but share that with the grocery store cashier.

I keep seeing God working in the grocery checkout line. As convenient as self-checkout is, I started gravitating toward going to where a person is and letting them help me with my purchase. I feel God pulling me that way, gently and kindly.

I had to recently get a cashier's check (what even is that anyway?), so I went to the Publix across the street from me and went in cluelessly to grab one. I began chatting with the Publix cashier Amaya, and she told me how she had lived in Nashville all her life. She has one daughter and they live together and her daughter works in the music industry.

We talked about how proud she is of her daughter, how the city has changed so much in her lifetime, and why can't rent prices just stay the same? We laughed and laughed and I finally had to go. We both said we were so glad to meet each other and how we hoped to see each other again.

Somehow this has become a pattern. I am becoming immersed in conversation with every cashier I meet at the grocery store. I used to jump to the ever-convenient self-checkout, but now I stand in line waiting for the next cashier available just to have that moment of connection on a Tuesday morning picking up groceries.

We have become reliant on technology and convenient devices to make our lives easier, and in turn, we have removed the ability to connect with other humans that we would not find in our everyday spheres of life.

Sometimes vulnerability feels easier with complete strangers. Nothing to lose, just a moment together knowing our paths may never cross again.

On Saturday afternoon I found myself standing in the Nordstrom dressing room trying on a few fall dresses. I was in search of a few new clothing items, a little treat to myself. I couldn't wait to see what I could find. While browsing the racks in Nordstrom, this bubbly saleswoman about my age started chatting with me and helping me find dresses to try on.

I would just be beginning to put on one dress when she would stop by with another. Usually, I do not want any assistance from retail employees while shopping, but I didn't mind her helping me for some reason. She seemed very genuine and passionate about fashion and she had a kindness about her.

When dropping off yet another dress to try, she looked at me and said, "Are you a Christian?" It took me by surprise and told her that I was, very curious about where this conversation could be leading. She replied, "Me too! My name is Biz. I noticed your cross necklace and thought maybe you were. I just moved to town and would love to be friends. Would you ever wanna get dinner or coffee sometime?"

I was blown away by her boldness. Next thing I know, we are sitting across the table from each other at Greenery Co. eating chipotle shrimp bowls and getting to know each other.

I want to be that vulnerable, risking potentially being rejected for the sake of getting to know someone. The hard part is sometimes it goes wrong. We put ourselves out there only to be met with a slammed door. But we have to keep trying. Being bold as Biz is the kind of person I want to be.

Tonight, I sat in a room with a handful of girls I have virtually nothing in common with except a mutual best friend. Our mutual friend was having a girls' night and had invited me over. These girls are all close friends, spending most of their free time together. I was tempted to cancel because I didn't want to feel like an outsider. I didn't want to have to force my way into conversation or feel uneasy because we live our lives differently and I feel strange sharing much with them.

But I went anyway because I didn't have to be an outsider. I am at a place where I finally feel confident enough in myself to acknowledge the feeling of not belonging and showing up anyway. I engaged the best I could in conversations that I didn't know what was being talked about. I asked questions, but I didn't try to force anything. I was there, painting an ornament, eating snacks, trying my best to just be there for my friend. Even when it felt uncomfortable.

I drove back to my house in the drizzling rain, grateful for the growth of showing up in spaces of all different shapes and sizes and still knowing I belong because I know and love who I am becoming and who I already am.

This whole book is one 60,000-word collection of some of my most vulnerable thoughts and moments. For the majority of my life, I have kept most shreds of vulnerability locked away in an inaccessible safe. But I feel safer now in a way that doesn't always make sense. I show up and risk getting rejected and feeling dumb and wondering what everyone is thinking about me, but slowly, very, very slowly, I'm reclaiming the person God created me to be.

So here I am, giving you, the reader, all I can possibly offer up. I hope it's good, and I hope it helps, but I am just proud I've gotten to the point where I can let you in on all of this. This isn't who I've always been, but it's who I am going to strive to be.

Chapter 18

DISCOVER DELIGHT

Growing up, my house was right next to a lot full of thick, tall trees and a tiny creek running through the backside of it. One day, my neighbors and I were playing on our trampoline and the soccer ball we were playing with went over the net and our fence and into the ominous woods. All of us were scared to go get the ball. The woods were this scary, dark place where we had yet to venture, but we were certainly not done playing our game. So we linked arms and walked over to the woods together. And that's when we realized how much fun the woods could be.

We had unbridled imaginations and were constantly playing out stories we created ourselves. The woods became the perfect place for us to continue to run wild with our stories. In our whimsical woods, there was a tree that appeared to be perfectly in the shape of a hook. I still to this day have never seen anything like it; it was as if it had begun to fall over but continued to grow regardless of its wonky shape.

So we named it Captain Hook Tree. And if you stood on it and closed your eyes, it would take you to Neverland. My sister, our neighbors, and I would jump on the tree and transport ourselves to an alternate world and play all day in Peter Pan's reality. As kids, the four of us were a creative bunch coming up with hours and hours of stories we would live out.

I don't know why I don't try and find the splendor in the everyday, ordinary things just because I'm now older. Some people would have looked at that tree and thought something was wrong with it, but we in our childlike mindsets saw something more exciting, something original. Something God created and called it good.

Our minds are tricky places. We believe what we want to believe and we see what we want to see. What if we chose to see the extraordinary in the ordinary? I bet we'd find joy a lot easier on days that feel monotonous. I want to live a little more like that, seeing trees that look like they belong to Captain Hook and remembering God's hand in all of it.

———

I am an extremely efficient person who loves schedules and a to-do list. I want every hour mapped out with a plan. Why waste time? With only 24 hours in a day, I have things to do!

But I seem to be surprised every day that my schedule can and will get thrown off. When I was handed the keys to my very own one-bedroom apartment, I could not wait to decorate and design it just the way I wanted. I mapped out a schedule of what needed to be done.

- Sweep the floors
- Wipe down countertops
- Vacuum
- Put together a buffet stand
- Roll out the rug

And last but certainly not least, put together the patio chairs. I had zero concerns in the world when it came to this task. I had pieced the patio table together earlier and it only took me about fifteen minutes. I had also built a buffet stand that was truly in one million pieces. These chairs would be a walk in the park.

The instructions said it might take me thirty minutes to put the pieces together for the chairs. Please. It took me three hours to build the buffet. I was not even slightly worried.

The instructions said I would need two people to build this, but that is what all the instructions said on each of the items before. So again, whatever. Let's do this.

I laid out all of the pieces and started sorting what goes together. The first step: attach Part B to Part D. Easy enough. I started putting these two pieces together, but the instructions weren't very clear about which end of each piece was up or down, left or right. I twisted them every way, knocking myself in the shins a few times before I finally figured it out. Okay, not bad.

Onto screwing the bolts in. I grabbed the Allen wrench and screw #1 and started twisting it in. It was pretty tough to twist the Allen wrench around, but I would not give up. Finally, it was done. I sat the two pieces up and then realized I had indeed screwed the seat in upside down. Ugh. I unscrewed and flipped around to try again.

One piece down. I continued to the next piece. The same thing happened again. I screwed in the leg upside down. My left thumb and pointer finger were already swollen and beet red from all of the twisting and turning. I laid down on my rug in defeat and to catch my breath. I started again.

Three hours later, I was staring at two chairs that were a little wobbly and had screws not all the way screwed in, just hanging out of the chairs. This was the best I could do and I wanted nothing more to do with these chairs ever again in my entire life.

As I lay on my rug staring up at the ceiling, trying to not think about how much hatred I had in my heart for those patio chairs, I thought about two things:

1. I'm really grateful rugs come just as they are and need no further attention.

2. My life has felt a little like the assembly of those patio chairs.

God has given me the pieces I need to assemble my life; He has been so generous in handing me all the different parts necessary to create something beautiful. I just need the courage, patience, and willingness to try and begin again if needed.

Life is frustrating and confusing and I wish these chairs would assemble themselves, but we weren't meant to run on autopilot. It's trial and error and new beginnings and a pot full of new ingredients changing the flavor of our lives over and over. It's impossible to figure out, but what I'm learning is we weren't meant to become masters of our lives. We were made to surrender our lives to the One who knows better and treasure Him more because of the sweet freedom His love brings each of us.

As I've put together my apartment piece by piece, I see little slivers of me weaved throughout what I've placed on the shelves and stuck to the refrigerator. Pictures of my friends scattered across the fridge to remind me of their happiest moments coming up: weddings and babies and all of life's big moments. My cream-colored built-in bookshelf has a row of just photos of me and my favorite people. I feel so lucky to be known and loved by some good, good people.

I have assembled my life, piece by piece, with people I love, a job I adore, and a God that I've surrendered my all to and I delight in knowing. Being in your 20s is so weird but so fun all in the same breath. I don't have it all figured out, and the more I try to know, the more I drown in expectations.

———

When I first moved to Nashville, my friends and I lived in this funky house that eventually was known as the Brightwood House. At Brightwood, you never know what you might find, it certainly was never dull. Once, I was headed to a job interview and went to open the front door to head to my car. As I turned the rickety gold doorknob, it fell onto the floor. Stunned, I picked it up and tried to finagle it back onto the handle with no luck. I could not get the door to open without the knob, so I was left with no other choice. I ran through our house, late for my interview, went out the back door, ran through our overgrown backyard to our fence's gate, then ran some more down our alley, and then down the street to my car. I am grateful that I didn't see a soul when this all happened.

This house had its issues, but one takes the cake. One night, I was sound asleep when I heard a loud crash. I woke up, startled, thinking someone was breaking in. I am severely disappointed in my fight or flight skills because I laid in my bed too terrified to move instead of getting up to see what caused this alarming sound.

A few minutes passed, and I didn't hear anything else so I just assumed I had a nightmare that felt too real and went back to sleep.

The next morning, I got out of bed and had forgotten about the whole incident. As I walked into our kitchen to grab breakfast, I paused as I noticed our kitchen ceiling was now lying on the floor.

I wasn't really sure what to do in this situation as I was a rookie when it came to having your ceiling lying on the floor, so my first thought was to go rescue my roommate whose room was upstairs. I didn't want her to fall through the ceiling! Now my fight or flight skills were really kicking in.

I went and told Brooke that she had to get up NOW! Unfortunately, it was a Saturday and I don't think she was too happy with me, understandably. I was just trying to save her life, you know?

She walked downstairs and couldn't believe that I was right: our ceiling lay in ruins on our kitchen floor. I called our landlord who didn't believe me either. He sent over our maintenance crew (who we had grown very familiar with amidst our ever-growing list of problems with this house), and our dear maintenance man didn't believe me either until he saw it with his own eyes. He said a few expletives, helped me clean up the mess and basically put a rather large black tarp band-aid on it until someone else could come take a look.

Until further notice, Brooke needed to shower downstairs, which meant FOUR girls would be sharing one shower. Fun, special times. Did I mention this went on to last a month? A month of sharing a shower and a month of having a gaping hole in our ceiling. It became an ever-running punch line with our friend group and even with acquaintances from the Internet. Our ceiling (or lack thereof) grew a little famous. We made the best we could of what we had in that house that was hanging on by a thread.

I have started coming home from work and trying to jot down joy bombs from the day, small moments that made me smile. I want more moments that make me laugh like that, seeing my ceiling on the floor. Here are a few of my favorite moments from the past few weeks:

▸ My intern at work bought orange balloons at Party City. He had the balloons inflated at the store and when he walked outside most of the balloons slipped out of his hand and floated away. He could not stop giggling about it.

▸ I asked a kid at work if she was having a fun day and she didn't answer. Instead, she paused for about ten seconds, and proceeded to ask me, "Is Dolly Parton still alive?" I would have to agree that this question matters more. We love you, Dolly.

▸ I have a new 3rd-grade friend at work who always comes back to hug me before she goes to her counseling session. She says very little else, but always, always, always makes sure she sees me before going on about her day.

▸ My very favorite kindergartner in the world came to hang out with me at work while her sisters were in counseling sessions. She brought me a lunchbox that included a sandwich with no crust, grapes, pretzels, and cheese. We made a thankfulness chain out of a rainbow of construction paper.

Delight doesn't come naturally, so I am looking for reminders everywhere about why delight matters and how I can make it what I search for first instead of looking for what's going wrong in the world around me. I need to claim joy before another feeling claims me.

———

I haven't always been someone to give something up for Lent. But a few years ago, I decided that what I wanted to give up was a sliver of my time every day. It wasn't going to be a lot, but it was going to be something. I wanted to cultivate a heart of gratitude after lots of negativity running through my mind, so I decided for 40 days I was going to write a letter to one person each day that I was grateful for.

40 people? Did I even know 40 people I would want to write a letter to?

The first few weeks were easy. I wrote notes to my family members, best friends, and roommates. But as I dwindled down on people that I was closest to, I asked God to bring people to mind that had impacted my life in all of its various stages. Day by day, I had someone new. One of these people was a friend from middle school. Another was an acquaintance from college. I wrote and wrote notes of thankfulness for each person and when I reached 40 notes I realized I still had so many I wanted to write!

We are conditioned to be people who grumble instead of people who live in gratitude. I didn't even know how many people I loved and was loved by until I spent time daily thinking through whom I could show gratitude to.

Delight is here and it is ours for the taking, but sometimes we need to take baby steps toward it. We zoom out on the big picture to the point that we lose sight of what joy, hope, and gratitude mean anyway. Starting small is a lot bigger than we know. We need moments that make us step back and seek out what really matters.

You may recall me talking about my furry co-worker named Happy Meal, Happy for short, earlier in the book. Happy is a vibrant one-year-old Golden Mountaindoodle therapy dog. As I'm sitting here on my lunch break doing a bit of writing, Happy is spending her lunch break with me while her mom is in a meeting. She is not super thrilled about this arrangement. She is pacing all around our office, whimpering like someone has stomped down on her foot. I keep calling her over, trying to soothe her, but it's the funniest thing. Every time she walks past me, she has the biggest smile on her face. She is crying and smiling all in the same breath.

The past year has taught me both can be true. We can be happy while hurting; we can seek delight in the mundane. We can know joy while feeling sorrow.

Lots of big feelings can exist together. My big emotions get away from me more often than not. It's easy to see the bad and feel like no good could possibly be left. But it's there, glimmering, shining, a light on a hill that can not be covered. He's there, my Jesus, showing me there is more to life than what I am told daily. He would not have created me if He did not have great purpose and intention for my life and yours too, my friend.

I want to live in delight. I want to be so immersed in the feeling that it just becomes who I am. I want to discover it daily: on a hard day of work, at lunch with a new friend, or on a long solo road trip with nothing beautiful in sight.

I know it's like a gold mine, sifting through to decipher what's a rock and what's something far more valuable. I want to choose sifting over sitting and waiting for life to happen to me. We will never find delight if we wait for it to find us.

I want to uncover what God has for me. He's embedded a purpose in me and into you too. We're humans with beating hearts and a life worth delighting in no matter the circumstance. As we grow into grown-up versions of ourselves, I pray that you and I see His hand in all of it. I can't think of something more worthy of delighting in.

Conclusion

A CONFETTI-FILLED LIFE

I adopted a cat named Confetti. She is an explosion of orange, white, black, and brown fur topped off with the daintiest pink nose you've ever seen. I had debated getting a cat for a long time. I desperately wanted a furry friend to return home to after work each day, and a cat felt like the best fit for my one-bedroom apartment life. I spent dozens of hours contemplating it, staring at pictures of cats on Facebook, and researching all that it takes to have a pet.

I was home recently for a long weekend with my parents. I met them at a local favorite, Taco Loco, and was munching on some chips when I nonchalantly asked my mom, "Would you want to go to the animal shelter after lunch with me to look at cats?" I didn't expect a yes. I had driven straight from Nashville to the restaurant and had no idea what her plans were for the day.

Next thing I knew, my mom and I were standing in a room with two dozen silver crates holding cats and kittens of all ages and sizes.

I walked by each crate admiring how many beautiful cats there were at the shelter. I giggled a little when I saw this tiny cat with the name "Confetti" attached to her crate. I opened the door and she immediately came out to greet me and was a real friendly girl. I loved her instantly, but I wanted to keep meeting all the other cats.

I had started playing with Confetti's neighbor when I felt a tap on my shoulder. I turned to find Confetti's paw nudging me over and over through the silver bars as if saying, "Come back here lady! You will love me!"

And that's all it took. I scooped her up, filled out the paperwork, and we went home.

We've been together for three weeks now. Her first night sleeping in my apartment, I woke up to find her nuzzled under my chin, with no room for any sudden movements. We became the best of friends, no questions asked, no doubt in either of our minds, instantaneously.

I have three years left in my twenties. I don't think I'll be sad when my twenties are over; I feel like I'm just getting started, just waking up to who God created me to be. I hope when I'm 30, I will be a little less of an overthinker, not needing every single minor detail to make a decision. Whether it's getting a cat or a couch or a condo or a coffee. I want my life to be filled with confetti popping all around me, celebrating my friends, my Savior, my best moments, my life. I hope I'll live a little freer, be a little less hard on myself, love a little harder, and laugh a little louder. It won't be perfect, and I'm okay with that. Life will never be what it once was and there is such beauty and some sorrow that comes with life changing.

That cul-de-sac I grew up on was no dead end, it was just the beginning of a life full of purpose, passion, hope, hurt, and healing. With each crossroad I face, I am reminded that I may not always know where I'm headed, but I know who I'm going with, to whatever is next. I hope my life will radiate joy, celebrating every small and big moment, giving thanks for what my life has become. I couldn't have dreamed it up, but God did. And I believe He's working for my good in this crazy decade of life. I believe He's refining me and restoring me and He's making me new. Even if I don't feel that some days, I believe it. He's raining down confetti in my life, an explosion of color on my grayest of days. I want to be more like Him.

REFLECTION QUESTIONS

CHAPTER 1 - GETTING LOW ENOUGH TO GET JESUS

1. What does having faith look like in your own life?

2. Do you feel like you need a shift in your life and if so, what does that shift need to be? Who can you invite into this conversation that will help hold you accountable?

3. Has there been a defining moment in your life where you've been the lowest you've ever been? What has happened on the other side of that moment and how has that shaped your faith?

4. The story about the woman on the Greyhound bus highlights the importance of connection in overcoming addiction. How have relationships and connections played a role in your own challenges or triumphs? Any memories come to mind?

5. When you're in murky waters, what helps you maintain faith despite not having all the answers?

CHAPTER 2: SPENDING TIME WITH JESUS

1. What is your rhythm for spending time with Jesus? Do you have a structure or do you just hope for the best and see what happens daily?

2. What is one topic or book of the Bible you want to commit to spending more time in or learning more about? Check out Bible studies that cover that topic

and jump in! I recommend looking into Precept studies. I also am a huge fan of Beth Moore and Priscilla Shirer's Bible studies!

3. Consider the condition of your heart. Do you find yourself planting seeds in rocky ground or good soil? How has this impacted your spiritual growth?

4. Do you view yourself as a believer or a disciple of Jesus? (It's okay if you feel more like a believer than a disciple. It changes every day for me, but I'm hoping to move toward being a disciple more and more each day.)

5. How do you like to spend time with Jesus? Through worship, prayer, a Bible study? How can you structure your time with Him to be more about quality of time than quantity of time?

CHAPTER 3: GRANDMOTHERS WHO PRAY

1. Get out a pad of sticky notes and write down a few prayers on individual sticky notes. Tape them to a wall in your home that you pass frequently. Pray over the words you've written and watch as God answers them. Tape His answers to your prayers up too. It'll encourage you on the days that you feel like giving up. God's not done working yet.

2. Do you feel the freedom to pray to God anywhere? This week, spend your commute to work with the radio off and just talk to God and listen to Him.

3. Find a day this month when you can spend 4 hours praying. Yep, a whole morning or afternoon. Check out resources like the One Hour Prayer Cycle to help you get started. Leave your phone in your car or your backpack and pray, walk around a park and just listen to God, read your Bible, and just spend time with Him.

4. Do you have people in your life, grandparents, parents, best friends, who you know pray for you? How can you show your gratitude for their prayers today? (If you don't have someone in your life who prays for you, I would love to be that person. Email your prayers to me at maryspencerveazey@gmail.com and I would be honored to pray for you.)

5. Do you have places or times where you feel that it's easier to connect with God in prayer? How do you create space for prayer in your daily life?

CHAPTER 4: INVEST IN A LOCAL CHURCH

1. What are your non-negotiables when it comes to the church you choose to be a part of? What are your preferences?

2. If you haven't found a church to call home yet, what are 3-5 churches you'd like to try? Make a list, look up their services, and create a plan to visit them in the next month or two. Invite a friend to go with you!

3. If you have found a church home, what is one way you want to invest more deeply? Through volunteering with the kids' ministry? Getting plugged into a Bible Study? Becoming a greeter for a service on Sundays? Connect with a member of church leadership to find out how you can best serve.

4. How do you navigate differences in beliefs within your friends who are also Christians? Do you talk about why you believe what you believe or are you more prone to keep what you think to yourself?

5. How has or can being a part of a church community enrich your life and relationships? What can you give and what can you potentially receive?

CHAPTER 5: THE POWER OF MENTORSHIP

1. Who do you already have in your life that is or can be a mentor to you? Write down who that person is. Can you begin to reach out to them every month to get coffee or lunch with you?

2. What gaps do you feel are missing in your career that you could seek advice and wisdom from someone who's been there? Talk to your friends who are older than you about someone that they may know who could be good for you to meet.

3. Who would you say is on your Board of Directors? What are their roles and what do they contribute?

4. Who have been or currently are mentors you have that have made an impact on your life throughout the years? Write them a card or give them a call today to show your appreciation for them.

5. What has been a significant professional decision you've had to make in your career that you have or wish you had sought guidance on? What would you do differently moving forward, especially by having a mentor on your team?

CHAPTER 6: SABBATH – A GIFT FOR YOUR SOUL

1. Does resting with your hands or resting with your mind feel like a greater need in this current season?

2. How can you rest with either your hands or your mind on your day of rest?

3. What day could you Sabbath this week? What will that look like for you and who can you tell to hold you accountable? And don't beat yourself up if you don't do it perfectly... I most certainly never do it quite right. But I'm trying!

4. What are three ways you can rest on your Sabbath? (Deleting your social media apps for the day, not taking out the trash, leaving off the TV, etc.)

5. How can you develop a Sabbath mindset in your daily routine? In what ways can you build in small moments of rest throughout your day and week?

CHAPTER 7: BODY AS A TEMPLE - PHYSICALLY AND EMOTIONALLY

1. How do you view your body? What has influenced you when it comes to the way you view your body? (celebrities, friends, the way you heard people talk about their bodies growing up, etc.)

2. What form of exercise seems to make the most sense for your life and is something you enjoy doing? How many days a week could you commit to moving your body?

3. What were your perceptions of counseling growing up? What do you believe about counseling today?

4. Do you feel like counseling is a resource you need in your life currently? Why or why not? It's okay if not, but know it is not nearly as scary or intimidating as it might seem.

CHAPTER 8: CAREERS

1. If you've already entered the workforce, what are three takeaways you have from your first job that have helped you know what to look for in future jobs?

2. If you're still in high/school or college, when you think about a job that you would find joy and purpose in, what does it look like?

3. If you're thinking about looking for a new job, who are two mentors or friends you could connect with to talk more about what you're looking for? Send them a text right now asking them to get coffee or lunch in the next two weeks.

4. Who are three friends, family members, mentors, or co-workers you could send a message or call and encourage them in the work they do every day? Reach out to them today.

5. Think about your current job— what do you think your purpose is in your role? Why do you think your job matters? (And if you don't feel like it matters, I promise you it does. No matter what it is.)

CHAPTER 9: THE THIEF OF JOY

1. When do you find yourself comparing yourself to others

the most? When looking through social media? At school? When you're at a party with friends?

2. Think of one person you tend to compare yourself to. What if you assumed the best about them and the best about yourself too?

3. How can you cheer on the person you listed above today? Could you send them a text of encouragement, comment on their latest post, or even talk to them about the comparison you feel rearing up sometimes?

4. Who can you talk to when you feel yourself running toward comparing yourself to others?

5. How can you cultivate a belief about what's true when it comes to your inherent worth and identity, and what role does faith play in that process?

CHAPTER 10: HOBBIES

1. What is a sport, activity, or hobby you wish you had done as a child? Sign up for lessons today!

2. Where in your week could you consistently make time to do something that feeds your soul as a hobby does?

3. What hobby could you do with a friend? Schedule time once a month to do a fun activity with a friend!

4. What hobbies could you incorporate into your Sabbath? What hobbies would feel restful to you?

5. What's a hobby you've tried but didn't enjoy? Why didn't you enjoy it? What's an activity that you love but

rarely make time for? How could doing more of what you love change your week and your life?

CHAPTER 11: TRYING TO TRUST GOD

1. Do you think societal norms influence how you cope with loss, and how does it play out in your life or community?

2. Are you at a place where you feel like the pieces of your life are crumbling around you? If so, what has fallen apart? If not, when was the last time you felt like things were really hard?

3. When times are tough, does the scale tip more toward grief or joy or is there a good balance? What action steps could you take today to be proactive in keeping the scales tipping back to joy?

4. In what ways do you not trust God? Why do you think that is?

CHAPTER 12: YESES, NOS, & BOUNDARIES

1. What are areas or situations in your life where you feel God calling you to say yes but you don't want to?

2. What about areas that you feel God calling you to say no? Talk to a trusted friend, mentor, or your Bible study group about this.

3. What are boundaries that you have a hard time setting in your life?

4. What is one boundary you can put in place today that you can continue to keep? (Less time on your phone by putting your phone up at 9 pm every night, deleting the number of an ex that you shouldn't keep speaking to,

leaving work at 5 pm instead of staying up until midnight working, etc.)

CHAPTER 13: FRIENDS – FINDING THEM, KEEPING THEM, AND LETTING THEM GO

1. Who are two acquaintances in your life you wish you had a deeper friendship with? Text them and ask to get dinner or coffee in the next two weeks and build on y'all's friendship!

2. Who are the friends in your life that are always worth fighting for? Why does their friendship matter to you?

3. If you don't have those friends in your life yet, keep showing up in spaces where you think those friends might be. Where are the places you can keep showing up in to hopefully meet those friends?

4. What friendship have you had to let go of that hurt and why did the friendship end? Is there a friendship in your life currently that is doing more harm than good?

5. Who are your literal neighbors? Do you know them? If you do, invite them over for dinner or coffee in the next two weeks. If you don't know your neighbors, grab a pack of cookies from the store and go introduce yourself tomorrow!

CHAPTER 14: DATING IN A DIGITAL WORLD

SINGLE FRIENDS:

1. What are the qualities you are looking for in a future spouse? List out everything that comes to mind.

2. Is there someone in your life that has the qualities that are on your list? A guy best friend or someone in your Bible study? Ask your friends to set you up with someone that might fit the qualities you are looking for!

FRIENDS THAT ARE DATING:

1. What are the doubts you have about your relationship?

2. Do you feel yourself comparing your relationship to the other relationships you see on social media? Take some time to reflect. How well do you know the people you are comparing your relationship to? If it would be helpful, consider muting friends that you are comparing yourself to or unfriend those you don't know that well.

FRIENDS THAT ARE MARRIED:

1. Who are three friends you know who are single? Talk with your husband and see who you could set them up with. Keep a running list in your Notes app of you and your spouse's single friends and actively think about people you could set up.

2. Reach out to your friends who are in relationships and check-in. If they open up to you about current frustrations in a relationship (or even lack thereof) ask how you can be praying and share with them current struggles in your life.

CHAPTER 15: SINGLENESS IN YOUR TWENTIES

1. What are you doing to actively meet and get to know new people if you're single? Hanging out with the same three friends is amazing, but it may not lead you to new opportunities, new friendships, or even new relationships.

2. How are you grateful for this time being not yet married?

CHAPTER 16: FINANCES AND GIVING

1. In what ways do you currently budget?

2. How often do you want to budget? Weekly, daily, bi-weekly? Commit to a schedule for three months and see how it shifts your spending and saving.

3. If you're a Christian, do you currently tithe? No shame if you don't, but what would it look like to set up tithing to your church automatically so you are committed to giving consistently?

CHAPTER 17: VULNERABILITY

1. How do you show up and be vulnerable with the people in your life? How do you show a shred of vulnerability with strangers you cross paths with in your everyday life?

2. When do you feel most comfortable opening up to others? Do you have trusted voices in your life (friends,

counselors, family members) with whom you feel like you can share hard things?

   a. If so, what would it look like to call or text one of them today and thank them for being a safe space and person for you?

3. Is vulnerability uncomfortable for you or have you grown more accustomed to it? How do you dodge vulnerability? Do you dodge with humor, avoidance, or aggression?

4. Do you find yourself favoring convenience over connection in your everyday life? What's a step you can take today to move toward connection over convenience? (Skip self-checkout at the grocery store and wait in line or go to the bookstore and chat with the employees instead of ordering books on Amazon!)

5. What is or was the most important lesson you learned in your twenties about vulnerability? Share it on Instagram

and tag me @mencervz. I want to hear what you have to say!

CHAPTER 18: DISCOVER DELIGHT

1. How can you practice and cultivate a heart of gratitude daily? Spend five minutes a day living out gratitude whether it's calling an old friend and telling them how much they mean to you or spending time in prayer thanking God for all the small and big moments you are grateful for today.

2. What are some joy bombs currently in your life? Write down a list of three joy bombs, and share them with your friends on social media! Tag #CCJoyBombs so I can see them.

ACKNOWLEDGMENTS

My heart is overwhelmed with gratitude for so many incredible people who have helped, supported, and loved me as I've written this book. I'll never be able to include all of the people that I want to thank, but I sure am going to try my best.

Mom and Dad - from day one you have encouraged me to go after what I want and feel like I'm made for, and in turn, it's created a spirit in me that is rarely afraid to just go for it. Whatever that "it" is. You both mean the world to me and I have to stop here because I'll start crying if I don't!

Cam - my little sister who doubles as one of my best friends. You are a cheerleader and fierce protector of those you love. It's something I don't take for granted. Love you so much for cheering me on during all of my adventures. I know I will always be able to count on you and for that, I'm so grateful.

To the very first readers of my book - Charlotte, Kate, and Annie, your feedback, kindness, and thoughtfulness in your suggestions has helped make this book the best it could ever be. I am forever indebted to each of you for taking the time to be the first readers of my most vulnerable thoughts.

I always dreamed about writing a book, and I'm overwhelmed with gratitude for hope*books and everyone who helped make this happen - Kati, Charity, Brian, Hope, and so many more. Angela, thank you for being the best editor a girl could ask for. You helped me bring this book to life and made sure it made sense after so many nights writing after working long days.

A big squeeze of gratitude for my friends - my people in Nashville (Brooke, Jane, Leigh, Jacob, Brian, Shelly, Sally, Betsy, Jenna and so many more) and my people all over the country and world (Ally, Abby, Sarah, Emilie, Chelsea, Nikki, Kennedy, Sav, and Anna to name a few), thank you for cheering me on in this process and still being my friend when I was holed up in my apartment writing my life away. I don't know how I would get through life without each of you and I never want to find out.

To my grandmothers who pray - Meme, Grams, and Ms. Peggy (and my wonderful Grandanny who prays for me too!), I'm pretty sure your prayers launched me to this very moment. To have grandparents like each of you is one of the best parts of my life. To be so loved by each of you is a gift that never stops giving.

I cannot forget my Daystar people who have become my family over the past year- Aaron, Allye, Amy, Blair M, Blair W, Corrie, David D, David T, Don, Emma P, Emma S, Jenny, Katie, Kenneth, Mary, Melissa, Paige, Rachel, Richie, Shannon, Sherman, Sissy, Susan, and Tommy. I will never be able to believe that I get to work at a place as magical as Daystar. You all have changed my life and inspired me in ways I will never be able to put into words.

ACKNOWLEDGMENTS

Thank You, Jesus, for bringing me to this place for such a time as this.

To every single reader, thank you from the VERY bottom of my heart for reading *Cul-de-sac Crossroads*. I cannot believe I'm living in the moment that I so often prayed for. Thank you for encouraging me and reminding me why these words matter. Giving you all hugs in my mind!

To my Savior, I hope and pray this book glorifies You. Thank You for redeeming me and making me new. I could not make it through life without Your constant and steady hand guiding me. I love you, Lord.

NOTES

Chapter 3: Grandmothers Who Pray

1. *The one hour prayer cycle [youversion plan]*. Vision. (2021, December 27). https://zume.vision/reports/the-one-hour-prayer-cycle-youversion-plan/

2. Barnes, S. (2005). *The Art of Listening Prayer*. Praxis Press.

Chapter 6: Sabbath - A Gift for Your Soul

3. Downs, A. (2020, September 6). [Instagram post]. Instagram. https://www.instagram.com/anniefdowns/p/CEzAX_QjbW-/

4. Hilotin, J., & Infographics by Vijith Pulikkal, A. P. M. (2023, March 7). *Deadly scroll without end: How infinite scroll hacks your brain and why it is bad for you*. Special-reports – Gulf News.

5. Suess, Dr. *The Cat in the Hat*. Random House, 1957.

6. Millennials: The tired generation. Sleep Centers of Middle Tennessee. (2022, April 22). https://sleepcenterinfo.com/blog/millennials-sleep-deprived/#:~:text=The%20problem%20with%20

millennials'%20sleep,to%20the%20Pew%20Research%20Center

7. Moore, M. E. (2019). Core 52: A Fifteen-Minute daily guide to build your bible IQ in a year.

8. Quote. (n.d.-a). Eugene H. Peterson Quotes. https://quote.org/quote/if-you-dont-take-a-sabbath-something-271561

Chapter 7: Body as a Temple - Physically and Emotionally

9. Mayo Foundation for Medical Education and Research. (2023, August 26). *7 great reasons why exercise matters*. Mayo Clinic. https://www.mayoclinic.org/healthy-lifestyle/fitness/in-depth/exercise/art-20048389

10. Bendix, A. (2023, August 8). *Just 4,000 daily steps may lower your risk of death, study finds*. NBCNews.com. https://www.nbcnews.com/health/health-news/daily-steps-to-lower-risk-of-death-rcna98754

Chapter 8: Careers

11. Shirer, P. (2017). Week Five, Day 3: Timing is Everything. In *Discerning the voice of god: How to recognize when god speaks* (p. 149). essay, LifeWay Press.

12. City, R. C. to. (2024, April 19). *The missional disciple: Session 1 - work within the biblical narrative by Dennae Pierre*. Vimeo. https://vimeo.com/710538286/57ab5ad807?share=copy

Chapter 9: The Thief of Joy

13. Alhusseini, M. (2023, April 17). *Instagram sells 44 million blue checks in one day- that's $660 million!* Visionary Magazine. https://www.visionary-mag.com/post/instagram-sells-44-million-blue-checks-in-one-day-that-s-660-million

14. Carnegie, D. (1936). *How To Win Friends and Influence People*. Simon & Schuster.

Chapter 10: Hobbies

15. University, U. S. (2021, November 30). *How hobbies improve mental health*. USU. https://extension.usu.edu/mentalhealth/articles/how-hobbies-improve-mental-health

16. Lelean, J. (2021, February 15). *The science behind why hobbies can improve our mental health*. Connecting Research. https://research.reading.ac.uk/research-blog/the-science-behind-why-hobbies-can-improve-our-mental-health/

Chapter 11: Trying to Trust God

17. Stanley, C. F. (2014). *Every Day in His Presence*. Thomas Nelson.

Chapter 12: Yeses, Nos, & Boundaries

18. Amer, N. (2020, June 26). *How to use your experiences to build boundaries instead of walls*. Medium. https://nadiaadamamer.medium.com/how-to-use-your-experiences-to-build-boundaries-instead-of-walls-a825ddae7116

Chapter 13: Friends - Finding Them, Keeping Them, and Letting Them Go

19. Fileta, D. K. (2023). *Reset*. Harvest House Publishers.

Chapter 14: Dating in a Digital World

20. BlackRiver. (2022, March 8). *There are not enough tall men to go round*. Medium. https://medium.com/writers-blokke/there-are-not-enough-tall-men-to-go-round-91e29cf89ed1

21. DeMatteo, M. (2023, May 23). *The average American has $90,460 in debt-here's how much debt Americans have at every age*. CNBC. https://www.cnbc.com/select/average-american-debt-by-age/

22. Pino, I. (2023, December 18). *57% of Americans can't afford a $1,000 emergency expense, says New report*. Fortune Recommends. https://fortune.com/recommends/banking/57-percent-of-americans-cant-afford-a-1000-emergency-expense/

Chapter 17: Vulnerability

23. Brown, B. (2018). Rumbling with Vulnerability. In *Dare to Lead* (pp. 90–90). essay, Random House.

ABOUT THE AUTHOR

Meet Mary Spencer Veazey, a Georgia native known for infusing her writing with relatable and uproarious storytelling, coupled with profound truths about Jesus. She lives in Nashville, Tennessee, with her cat Confetti and is the Engagement Manager for Daystar Counseling Ministries. Mary Spencer is a proud graduate of both Auburn University (BA) and Belmont University (MBA).

Facebook: www.facebook.com/maryspencervz

Instagram: @mencervz

Website: www.maryspencerveazey.com

Substack: @maryspencerveazey

Interested in booking Mary Spencer to come speak about navigating your twenties with courageous clarity for your next event? Please email maryspencerveazey@gmail.com and let us know more about your event and how we might work together.

If you enjoyed *Cul-de-sac Crossroads*, would you please leave a review on Amazon and Goodreads? We cannot tell you how helpful reviews are for spreading the word about this book, and we would love to hear your feedback.

9 798891 850736